LIGHTEN UP

LIGH

A HEALTHY NEW WAY TO COOK

Photography by Petrina Tinslay

Quadrille

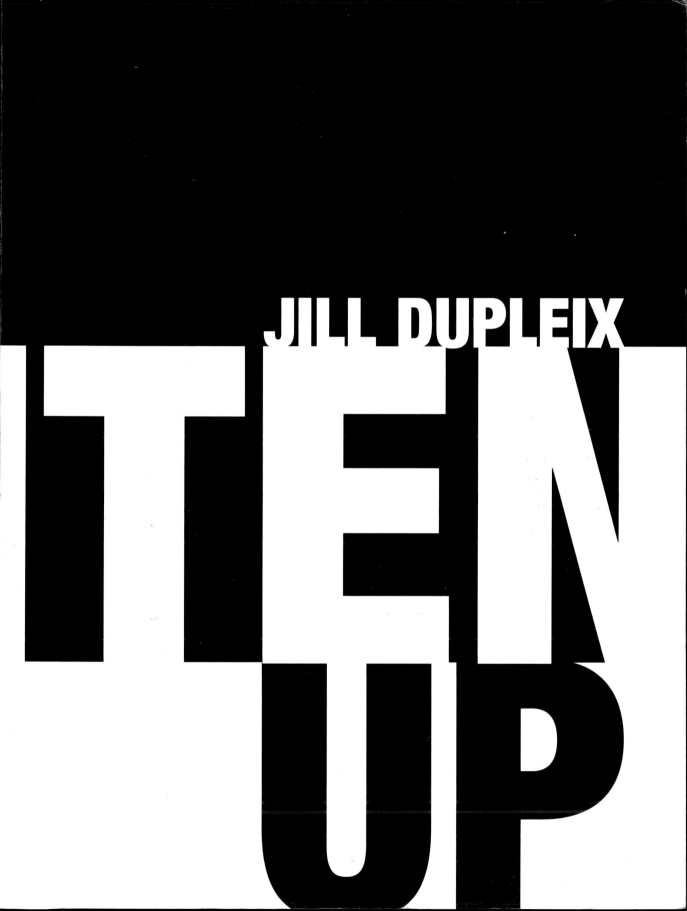

This is not a diet book or a nutrition-based regime – it's much more fun than that. This is a book of recipes for people like me who love their food but who want to be healthy. It's a way of moving your kitchen, your cooking and your eating to a lighter place.

Eating and drinking brings me enormous pleasure, and so does cooking and feeding people. But I also want to feel better when I get up from the table at the end of the meal than when I sat down.

Food lovers and health fanatics used to be two opposing groups but we are now, increasingly, on the same side, and saying the same thing. "Eat less, exercise more, drink water, and eat loads of fruits and vegetables." We all want to eat well, to look forward to our meals, and to have an extra glass of wine with dinner and get away with it for as long as humanly possible.

These days, we can take the best ideas that modern nutrition gives us, and the best produce available, and benefit from both. There is a vast amount of information available on diet and nutrition (sometimes too much), and good food is more accessible than ever before. We just need to be able to put it all together for ourselves on an everyday basis so that it works for our very busy lives. That's where I hope this book can help.

Over the last few years, the balance in my cooking has naturally shifted away from heavy meats to lighter fish, salads, grains, veggies and fruit. It's all about flavour, but without the cream, the pastry, and the animal fats. This is reflected in the book, so while there are recipes for red meat, pasta and puddings, there are more recipes for fish, soups, salads, vegetables, pulses, grains and fruit.

It's not just our food that could lighten up, it's our whole approach to cooking – the techniques and the tools we use, the key ingredients, and the final presentation. I've learnt all sorts of tricks along the way, like how to make the creamiest ice-cream without cream, eggs or sugar (with bananas); and how to use less oil when cooking (decant it to a plastic squeezy bottle, and always heat the pan first).

I love the clean flavours of modern food, the strong flavours of seasonal food, and the energy-giving qualities of healthy food. I want breakfasts to energise me, salads to revitalise me, soups to restore me, winter food to comfort me and desserts to refresh me. Food is all about pleasure, not punishment. Tea, coffee, red wine and dark chocolate are all good for us.

Terry's story My husband Terry is a restaurant critic who lives for food. He is quite simply the hungriest man I know. When I first met him, he took me out for lunch, which lasted until midnight. There was no going back after that. Together we threw ourselves into learning about food, wine, cooking, drinking, shopping and eating out. We were heavy users of food and drink, and we got away with it for a while…

I broke first, perhaps because there is more pressure on women to be slim, but I think it was really because I didn't have my old energy and feeling of lightness, and my digestive system was having a hard time coping with the richness of our diet.

So I very slowly started lightening up, eating food that was good for me and my tastebuds. My recipes, then running weekly in the Sydney Morning Herald and The Times in London, became lighter as well, and my regular readers soon noted the difference.

"I've lost interest in celebrity chefs with loads of saturated fats in their recipes", wrote one. "It's easy to make food taste good with cream. It is also socially irresponsible. It's time well regarded chefs moved on and started cooking in a responsible way."

She is right, of course, and I felt I was on the right track. But Terry still kept eating as if every meal was his last, until one day, he stood on the scales and nearly broke them. Looking at that arrow point to 18 stone 4lb

(116kg), he says, gave him the fright of his life. From that day on, he started choosing lighter, healthier food.

By having a proper breakfast, eating fewer carbs, falling in love with fish and walking every day, he slowly but gradually lost 6 stone (38kg), and has now happily settled on his ideal weight.

To this day he doesn't call what he did a diet, because, he says, it has never felt like one. He calls it a rethink, because he decided to eat for health rather than weight loss, knowing that if he succeeded in the first, the second would naturally follow. So things that had been staples (red meat, pasta, bread, potatoes) became occasional treats. Breakfasts that had been cereal and toast became porridge. Snack opportunities that had been sandwiches became crisp apples, nuts and bunches of grapes. Where there was wine, there was water as well.

His cholesterol and blood pressure settled, his skin looked much better, and he looked like the man I fell in love with all those years ago.

As he says, "I discovered that if you filled up on the good stuff, there wasn't room for the bad stuff." The real end result, however, is that the weight has stayed off because he retrained his brain and his tastebuds, to change lifelong (bad) habits and start new (good) ones.

What we learnt

- Eat for pleasure, flavour and health, not for weight loss.
- Start the day with oats. Eat porridge in winter and Swiss-style muesli in summer and you won't be hungry for hours.
- Eat more fish, chicken, salads and vegetables, and less red meat, pork, pasta and potatoes.
- Forget what your mother told you and don't finish everything on your plate.
- Beware of 4pm, when blood sugar levels dip. Snack on fruit and nuts instead of chocolate and crisps.
- It's not all about food. Walk instead of drive. Take the stairs instead of an escalator. Move instead of sit. Get enough sleep.
- When you eat bread, eat good bread – sourdough, wholemeal or rye.
- Don't cut anything out, just cut everything down.
- Steam instead of grill; grill instead of roast; roast instead of fry; and pan-fry instead of deep-fry.
- Drink better, drink less, and drink only with the evening meal.

I am not a nutritionist, and I don't see food in terms of its phytonutrients and bioflavanoids. So I decided against passing on all the nutritional information relating to the ingredients and recipes. I have done my homework and know what is good and bad, but I have never been able to eat certain foods – like kiwi fruit – purely because they are good for me. Therefore I really can't expect anyone else to either.

I don't eat avocado just because it's an excellent source of oleic acid, great for cardiovascular health; or seaweed salad because it's so high in minerals like calcium. I just love eating them.

Likewise, I don't want to feel guilty about food. I feel guilty about enough things already. So I make sure I eat well enough most of the time, then I can get away with a handful of chips, another glass of wine or a slice of chocolate cake when I want it without beating myself up about it. Nutritionists say that as long as you're eating moderately and well 80% of the time, you're allowed the rest of the time off, which sounds good to me.

Modern nutrition also teaches us that it's more important to eat good, real food than what the supermarkets call 'low-fat' food, because of the nature of the fat. Nuts, oily fish and avocado may be higher in fat, but it's a healthy fat that helps the body absorb other beneficial nutrients. Without the fat, you don't get the goodness. A lot of low-fat food has to be stuffed full of artificial sweeteners and salts to make it taste of anything at all.

Speaking of fat, you want to steer clear of the nasty trans fats found in hydrogenated vegetable oils and margarines. Where possible, replace saturated fats (those that are mainly solid at room temperature like cheese, cream, butter, and processed cakes and biscuits) with unsaturated fats. Of these, monounsaturated fat is found in olive oil, seeds and nuts, and polyunsaturated fat is in oily fish, vegetable oils, nuts and seeds.

It's also good to seek out organic food grown without the use of chemicals and additives. Pay extra for a little peace of mind and to support the farmers, and scrub all other fruits and vegetables before cooking.

Good things to know

- Be aware of the fact that as you get older, you can't keep socking away the same amount of food. It's just common sense.
- Know what you are prepared to eat less of, and what you are not. I can do without cream, for instance, but not red wine. Terry has discovered he can live without beer, but not without sausages.
- Be confident you can change. Old habits die hard, and so do unhealthy people. Changing your eating habits is a slow, gradual process, a journey.
- Eat at the table, never out of a box or from a bag — and preferably not while you are working, reading or watching television.

- Slow down and chew your food, to help your digestion, avoid bloating, and let the brain tell you when you've had enough.
- Remember that your stomach is only the same size as your fist.
- Drink lots of water. Sometimes we snack because we are thirsty, not hungry.
- Don't just eat, dine. Light candles, play music, drink from good glasses, and bring interesting things to talk about (not money).
- Don't play the blame game. Being grown-up means you can't blame anyone but yourself for what you choose to eat.
- It's much more fun going to a greengrocer, fishmonger or butcher than to a supermarket where there is nobody to chat to about the greens, fish, meat, or even the weather.
- Make it easy to be a good cook. Update your cookbooks, invest in well-made pots and pans, treat yourself to great olive oil, bread and wine. Make your kitchen a beautiful place to be.

People who love food and appreciate flavour are far better off than those who don't. We eat more seasonally, we buy the freshest produce, we have fun with it in the kitchen, we taste, smell and listen to our food, and we don't deprive ourselves. We have control over our own health and happiness, just because we like to cook. So our food makes us feel better, which is the way it should be.

MORNING FOOD

Breakfast is like money in the bank for your body – an investment in your day. Go without and you are ripping yourself off. My life only started working when I began having breakfast every morning. Now I'm too terrified to stop.

Porridge oats are one of the best ways to start your day because the energy you get from them is released slowly, so it lasts longer. Sometimes this is really annoying when there's something delicious to eat lurking around mid-morning and I can't face it because I'm still full from my porridge.

Make your porridge even better for you by seasonally adjusting it. Add extra seeds and grains in winter, and move to a light, fruity Swiss-style muesli when the days get warmer.

Even so, I'd get bored with oats every day of the year, so I take weekends off, and have toasted sourdough and a boiled egg, or a brunch of pancakes and fresh fruit, or smoked salmon and flat bread. Funnily enough, by the time Monday morning comes around, I'm craving my bowl of porridge as if it were chocolate cake.

Even on weekends, it's good to keep your options light rather than heavy. Save the fry-up for later – I have always thought it makes a far better supper anyway, with a glass of wine. Instead, smash some ripe avocado onto grilled wholegrain bread and squeeze on lime or lemon juice; cook an instant miso soup; drizzle raw honey over yoghurt and crunchy granola; whip up a spicy omelette; or crush a soft-boiled egg and feta cheese onto grilled pita bread.

I think it's even more important on a working day to make the time to sit down and eat at the table. It de-stresses you, so you digest food more easily, and can head off feeling both energised and relaxed. Try to have breakfast at a similar time each day – it's very reassuring for your body to know that the brain is in control of your day. If you really are on the run, then toss fresh fruit, yoghurt and a handful of porridge oats into a blender for a 'breakfast martini' that you can take away with you.

And don't fall for those commercial crunchy breakfast bars; they are usually loaded with sugar that will give you instant energy that runs out fast. Even granola has its share of oil and honey when it is oven-roasted – that's why we love it. So I use it as a crunchy sprinkle rather than sit down to huge bowls of it.

When in doubt, grab a banana instead. I reckon bananas have saved my life in 20 different countries. When I'm travelling and my body clock goes all haywire, I practically live on them to get me through. They seem to calm me down and fill me up at the same time, bless them.

CRUNCHY
granola

10 OR MORE SERVINGS

400g rolled (porridge) oats
3 tbsp sunflower seeds
3 tbsp sesame seeds
2 tbsp linseed (flaxseed)
100g almonds
100g walnuts or brazil nuts
100g dried shredded coconut
pinch of sea salt
4 tbsp honey or maple syrup
3 tbsp olive oil or hempseed oil
1 tsp ground cinnamon
½ tsp freshly grated nutmeg
100g dried cranberries
100g dried sultanas

Make up a jar of this crunchy, munchy granola and spoon it over fresh fruit and yoghurt for a fast energising breakfast. Or just store the unroasted dry ingredients in a jar and eat by the bowlful with milk or natural yoghurt.

LINE two baking trays with non-stick baking paper.
HEAT the oven to 150°C/Gas 2.
TOSS the oats, seeds, nuts, coconut and sea salt together in a large bowl.
WARM the honey, olive oil, cinnamon and nutmeg in a pan, stirring, until just melted.
POUR the liquid over the dry ingredients, tossing well.
SPREAD evenly on the trays.
BAKE for 20 to 30 minutes, shuffling everything around once or twice to prevent sticking.
REMOVE from the oven and cool.
ADD the dried fruits.
STORE in an airtight container for up to a month.

SUPER
porridge

8 SERVINGS

300g rolled (porridge) oats
100g barley flakes
100g rye or wheat flakes
50g wheatgerm
50g sesame seeds
25g sunflower seeds
25g linseed (flaxseed)

Power up your basic porridge with extra slow-release, energy-giving stuff from the local health food store – my mix changes all the time, but this is a favourite – and you'll be lucky if you're hungry again by lunchtime.

TOSS all the porridge ingredients together.
STORE in an airtight jar until ready to eat.

PORRIDGE FOR TWO:
MIX 75g super porridge with 350ml cold water in a heavy-based pan, stirring well.
ADD a pinch of sea salt.
BRING to the boil and give it a good stir.
DROP the heat to very low and simmer for 7 minutes until soft and creamy, stirring occasionally.
DIVIDE between two bowls.
SERVE with a little honey, maple syrup or brown sugar, sultanas, sliced banana, milk, or whatever you like.

SUMMER
porridge

SERVES 2

75g rolled (porridge) oats

1 green apple (unpeeled)

4 tbsp natural low-fat yoghurt

1 tbsp mixed linseed (flaxseed),
    sesame seeds, sunflower
    seeds, pumpkin seeds, etc

1 tbsp sultanas

1 ripe banana

This apple-based Bircher muesli was invented in 1887 by the genius Swiss dietician Maximilian Bircher-Benner, who believed that food should keep the body healthy. Add whatever fruit is around, and top with crunchy granola (page 12) if you like.

SOAK the porridge oats in 200ml water for 30 minutes (while you wake up, have a shower, etc).

GRATE the apple directly into a bowl, right through the core, pips and all.

DRAIN the oats and tip into the bowl.

ADD the yoghurt, seeds and sultanas and quickly toss.

SLICE the banana directly into the bowl and mix lightly.

DIVIDE between two bowls and eat.

BREAKFAST
burrito

SERVES 4

3 ripe tomatoes

10 cherry tomatoes (red or
   yellow)

½ red onion, finely sliced

2 tbsp coriander leaves

handful of rocket leaves

1 tbsp lime juice

dash of Tabasco or chilli sauce

sea salt and pepper

4 flour tortillas

200g smoked or cured salmon,
   sliced

1 ripe avocado

2 limes, halved

Weekends call for a breakfast upgrade and a bit of a treat – like this tortilla with smoked salmon. Fold it, roll it or leave it sunny side up. Avocado is so rich and creamy there is no need for sour cream or other fats.

CHOP the tomatoes; halve the cherry tomatoes.

TOSS with the sliced onion, coriander, rocket, lime juice, Tabasco, sea salt and pepper.

HEAT the tortillas in a dry fry pan until lightly toasted.

TOP each tortilla with furls of smoked salmon.

HALVE, peel and chop the avocado.

STREW over the tortilla with the tomatoes and leaves.

SERVE with limes for squeezing.

CHILLI OMELETTE
with coriander chutney

SERVES 2

6 eggs
1 mild green chilli, finely sliced
sea salt and pepper
1 tbsp vegetable oil
2 tbsp coriander leaves
1 tsp nigella seeds, roasted

CORIANDER CHUTNEY:

50g fresh coriander leaves
2 tbsp cashew nuts
1 tsp ground cumin
3 tbsp natural low-fat yoghurt

Omelettes are light, quick, and easy to throw together when you're only half awake – then toss in a bit of chilli and wake up even faster. Like any good breakfast, this makes a great lunch or fast supper as well, with warm Indian bread and a dollop of yoghurt.

MAKE the chutney: whiz the ingredients in a blender with a dash of water until smooth, season and chill.

WHISK the eggs, 3 tbsp water, most of the chilli and sea salt and pepper in a bowl.

HEAT half the oil in a non-stick omelette or small fry pan.

POUR in half the egg mix, tilting the pan to spread it.

COOK over medium heat until golden, pulling the edges in with a fork to let the runny egg spill over and cook.

SCATTER with coriander leaves.

FOLD the omelette while it is still a little oozy.

TURN out and make the second omelette.

SERVE topped with the coriander chutney, nigella seeds and a few chilli slices.

BREAKFAST
martinis

Smoothies and slushies are another way of getting the goodness of fruit, in drinkable form. For some reason, I find them even more appealing by thinking of them as breakfast martinis. These are two of my favourites.

SERVES 2

200g blueberries, plus extra to
  serve
200ml sweetened
  pomegranate juice
handful of ice cubes

SERVES 2

2 tbsp porridge oats
4 Medjool dates, pitted
100g natural low-fat yoghurt
100ml freshly pressed apple
  juice or orange juice
1 tbsp honey
handful of ice cubes
freshly grated nutmeg

POMEGRANATE SLUSH

CHILL two large martini glasses.

WHIZ the blueberries, pomegranate juice and ice cubes in a blender until smooth and icy.

POUR into glasses and scatter with blueberries.

WILD OAT SMOOTHIE

WHIZ the oats, dates, yoghurt, apple juice and honey in a blender until smooth.

ADD ice cubes and whiz again until smooth.

POUR into glasses and dust with nutmeg.

GREEK EGGS
with feta

SERVES 4

1 tbsp olive oil

20 cherry tomatoes, halved

4 slices sourdough or pita
bread

6 large organic free-range eggs

sea salt and pepper

75g feta cheese

1 tsp dried oregano

2 tbsp mint leaves, torn

Eggs make a fabulous weekend breakfast or brunch because they are so fast to cook, and you can throw in anything you like. Always cook eggs gently – the more they cook, the harder they are to digest.

HEAT the olive oil in a large fry pan and throw in the cherry tomatoes.

COOK over gentle heat for 5 minutes until softened.

START grilling the bread now (the eggs won't take long).

CRACK the eggs into the pan and season lightly.

SQUIGGLE each yolk with the tip of a knife to break it.

CRUMBLE the feta on top and scatter with oregano.

COOK until the whites are half-set, then push the eggs around in the pan with a wooden paddle until lightly set.

PILE the eggs onto the grilled bread.

SCATTER with sea salt, pepper and mint leaves.

MYKONOS
fruit cup

SERVES 4

600g mixed fruit (strawberries, cherries, peaches, apricots, melon)
150g raspberries
1 tbsp icing sugar

VANILLA YOGHURT:

300g thick Greek yoghurt
½ tsp vanilla extract
1 tbsp honey

This is the sort of healthy breakfast they get around to having in the late afternoon on the Greek island of Mykonos, after dancing on the beach all night. If it works for them, it will work for us.

HULL the strawberries; stone the cherries, peaches and apricots; peel and deseed the melon.
CUT these fruits into small pieces and toss well.
PURÉE the raspberries and icing sugar in a blender to make a sauce.
WHISK the yoghurt, vanilla and honey until smooth.
PILE the fruits into four tumblers to half-fill.
ADD a thick layer of vanilla yoghurt, almost to the top.
SMOOTH with the back of a spoon.
SPOON a thick layer of raspberry sauce on top.
SERVE with a long parfait spoon.

BERRY
pancakes

SERVES 4

110g self-raising flour
1 tsp baking powder
60g caster sugar
1 large egg
150ml milk
2 tsp butter
150g thick, Greek-style yoghurt
200g mixed berries
few small mint leaves

I find a lot of breakfast muffins and pastries so rich and sweet they should be desserts, or so heavy with bran they should be given to horses. That's why I love these light little pancakes, topped with fresh fruit and yoghurt.

SIFT the flour and baking powder together into a bowl.
ADD the sugar and mix.
BEAT the egg into the milk, then pour into the flour, whisking until it just comes together (don't over-mix).
HEAT the butter in a small non-stick fry pan.
ADD 2 tbsp of the batter and cook until golden, about 1 minute.
TURN and cook the other side, about 1 minute.
LIFT out and keep warm, while you add a little more butter to the pan and cook another 3 pancakes in turn.
SPOON some yoghurt onto each pancake.
ARRANGE the berries on top.
SCATTER with mint leaves and serve.

WINTER FRUITS
with orange ricotta

SERVES 4

200g dried figs, halved
200g dried apricots
2 tbsp dried cranberries or
   cherries
100g pitted prunes
2 tbsp sultanas
1 tbsp orange flower water
2 tbsp honey

ORANGE RICOTTA:

250g fresh ricotta
100g natural low-fat yoghurt
1 tbsp honey
1 tbsp orange zest, plus extra
   to serve
1 tbsp orange flower water
2 tbsp orange juice

This is great in winter when there's not much fresh fruit around. The only tricky thing is remembering to soak the fruits the night before. On a very cold morning, gently heat the fruit and let the creamy ricotta melt into it.

CUT the figs and apricots into thick slices.
MIX with the cranberries, prunes, sultanas, orange flower water and honey in a bowl.
ADD enough boiling water to just cover and stir well.
LEAVE overnight, until the fruit is plump and swollen.
BEAT the ricotta with the yoghurt, honey, orange zest, orange flower water and orange juice.
SPOON the fruits into serving bowls, saving the syrup.
TOP with a big spoonful of creamy orange ricotta.
DRIZZLE with the syrup and scatter with orange zest.

Never be without a banana. Brilliant for a quick burst of energy (why do you think tennis players scoff them between sets), they come perfectly wrapped, ready to eat and easy to digest. On the run? Have your **BREAKFAST IN A GLASS:** peel and slice 2 bananas and toss with a dash of lemon or lime juice. Peel and dice a ripe mango. Halve 2 passion fruit and scoop out the pulp and juice. Pile the bananas into two glass tumblers or plastic tubs. Top with a thick layer of natural yoghurt, then a layer of mango and another layer of yoghurt. Spoon the passion fruit on top and chill until needed. For 2.

How do you cool off in summer without resorting to those sickly sweet, additive-stacked ice-creamy things in the shops? You freeze **BANANAS ON STICKS** and turn them into (almost) all-day suckers that will help you keep your cool without piling on the kilojoules. Peel 2 large bananas and cut off each end to leave the longest possible 'straight' bit in the middle. Skewer the middle sections onto wooden popsicle sticks and freeze on a tray, then store in a plastic bag in the freezer until needed. Or dip in runny honey, roll in toasted shredded coconut and re-freeze. For 2.

BANANAS X4

Or start your day with a **BREAKFAST BANANA SPLIT:** bake 2 unpeeled large bananas at 200°C/Gas 6 for 30 minutes until the skin is black. Halve lengthways and top with a plop of thick natural yoghurt. Drizzle with honey, scatter with toasted walnuts or crunchy oven-roasted granola and eat while still warm. This also doubles as a quick pud: just add a drizzle of banana-friendly liqueur, such as Amaretto, Frangelico or Nocello (almond, hazelnut and walnut respectively). Or go troppo with a topping of palm sugar, a drizzle of coconut milk and a squeeze of lime juice instead. For 4.

When you're feeling hollow (generally around 4pm every day) or when you weren't planning on having a pud but suddenly feel like something sweet (generally every night), throw together an instant **BANANA BRUSCHETTA**. Lightly grill two thick slices of sourdough or fruit bread and spread with fresh ricotta. Pile 2 sliced bananas on top, add a handful of mixed berries and scatter with 2 tsp brown sugar. Place under the grill until glazed and golden, dust with icing sugar and eat piping hot. It may only be bananas on toast, but it tastes like banana bread-and-butter pudding. For 2.

SALAD FOOD

Salads aren't just for summer. I eat a green salad every single day of the year, right through the depths of winter, because I feel I need one then even more than I do in summer.

It's not just something on the side, but a proper course in its own right that I crave. Eaten after the main course, it gives my food enough time to reach my stomach and tell my brain I don't need seconds.

Just because something is called salad doesn't mean it's automatically healthy. I have a doctor friend who has dubbed the ubiquitous Caesar salad the 'seizure' salad, because it is so loaded down with creamy dressing and fried croûtons.

For me, a salad means something fresh, natural and seasonal. The variety of leaves alone makes shopping a dilemma. Which to have – the peppery bite of rocket, the savouriness of radicchio, the sweetness of mâche, or the feathery bitterness of frisée?

Then there is the salad as a meal. I'll turn anything into a salad if it stands still long enough – like the roast chicken, the salmon, the watermelon, and the bread and tomatoes in this chapter. I also like to 'saladise' non-salad dishes – anything to get more greens – by strewing rocket leaves over tomato and mozzarella pizza, pasta and hearty stews, letting them wilt in the heat. Or by tossing handfuls of baby spinach leaves into soups at the very last minute. This simple act really lightens up your food, makes it look great and adds a whack of freshness that a scattering of parsley can't provide.

Salads give us masses of flavour and goodness without loads of fat or carbs, but you can still add fresh cheese, eggs, nuts, seeds and grains for the protein that will turn them into a balanced meal. Shelled hemp seeds, or hemp nuts, for instance, are packed with minerals and proteins, with the perfect ratio of omega fats 3, 6 and 9. They sound a bit hippy, but taste so soft and nutty, that they are one of the most interesting new foods in my kitchen.

If you want to make great salads, get yourself a centrifugal salad spinner. First, cover the leaves in cold water in the spinner to freshen them up, then drain them and whiz to get rid of all water, so the vinaigrette can cling to the leaves.

The dressing is best made with a whisk and a big bowl, for total control. Add a spoonful of Dijon mustard to a good olive oil and good vinegar, season with sea salt and pepper and whisk to combine. Then thin it out with a dash of water or whatever white wine you are drinking, for a light dressing with heaps of flavour. Add the whizzed leaves, turn them over gently with your hands, and pile onto a big plate. Heaven.

SEAWEED SALAD
with edamame

SERVES 4

100g frozen edamame (baby
   soybeans)
50g mixed dried seaweed
1 cucumber, peeled
3 small pink radishes
100g baby rocket or spinach
   leaves
1 tsp black and white sesame
   seeds, toasted

DRESSING:

1 tbsp mirin (sweet rice wine)
2 tbsp grapeseed oil
1 tsp sesame oil
1 tbsp rice vinegar or lemon
   juice
½ tsp wasabi paste
sea salt

This is the salad of the 21st century, full of the minerally soft crunch and sea-bright goodness of seaweed. Buy little packs of mixed, dried seaweed (*kaiso salada*) from Japanese food stores, just add water, and toss into soups and salads.

COOK the frozen edamame in simmering salted water for 5 minutes, then drain and cool.

SOAK the seaweed in lukewarm water for 15 minutes, then drain.

SHELL the edamame and set aside.

SHAVE the cucumber lengthways with a veggie peeler into thin slices, then cut into matchsticks.

SLICE the radishes finely.

WHISK the dressing ingredients together in a bowl.

TOSS the rocket, radishes and edamame in the dressing.

SQUEEZE the seaweed and cucumber to get rid of any excess water.

ADD to the salad and toss lightly.

SCATTER with sesame seeds and serve.

SALMON, ORANGE
and chickpea salad

SERVES 4

600g salmon fillet, skin on,
  pin-boned
sea salt and pepper
1 orange
1 tbsp orange zest
2 tbsp orange juice
1 tsp lemon zest
1 tbsp lemon juice
2 tbsp olive oil
400g canned chickpeas, rinsed
handful of rocket leaves or mâche
3 tbsp small black olives
1 tbsp tiny salted capers, rinsed
2 tbsp mint leaves

This takes me back to the Amalfi coast in southern Italy, where the scent of oranges and lemons hang in the air, and the food is simple, beautiful and full of flavour.

HEAT the oven to 200°C/Gas 6.

PLACE the salmon on a foil-lined roasting tray.

BAKE for 10 minutes or until lightly pink inside.

REST for 20 minutes.

PEEL off the skin, break the juicy flesh into chunks with your fingers and season well.

CUT away the skin and pith from the orange, then cut the flesh into chunks.

WHISK the orange zest and juice, lemon zest and juice, olive oil, sea salt and pepper in a bowl.

ADD the salmon, chickpeas, rocket, orange segments, olives, capers and mint leaves, and toss lightly.

SERVE on a large share plate or four dinner plates.

SUMMER VEG
with goat cheese

SERVES 4

400g baby carrots, scrubbed
200g fine green beans, topped
200g podded broad beans
400g thin asparagus spears,
   trimmed
400g small courgettes (zucchini),
   sliced on the diagonal
2 baby fennel bulbs or spring
   (green) onions, trimmed
200g goat cheese
2 tbsp pistachios or pecans

DRESSING:

2 tbsp extra virgin olive oil
1 tbsp walnut oil
1 to 2 tbsp apple cider vinegar or
   lemon juice
sea salt and pepper

The best summer vegetables grow fast, are picked young and taste of sunshine. If you buy firm goat cheese in a log shape, add it by the slice. If it is soft and fresh, then just crumble it in with your fingers.

BRING a large pot of salted water to the boil.

COOK the carrots, green beans, broad beans, asparagus and courgettes for 4 to 5 minutes, picking them out of the water while still bright.

SLICE the baby fennel lengthways, or chop the spring onions into 3cm lengths.

ADD to the pot for 30 seconds only, then drain.

WHISK the dressing ingredients together in a bowl.

TOSS the warm vegetables in the dressing.

STREW on four serving plates.

ADD the goat cheese, scatter with pistachios and eat.

AVOCADO, SPINACH
and hemp seed salad

SERVES 4

2 firm ripe avocados

1 green apple

handful of live bean sprouts or
  cress

½ red onion, finely sliced

100g baby spinach, washed

1 tbsp shelled hemp seeds

1 tsp nigella seeds

1 tsp pumpkin seeds

DRESSING:

1 tbsp hemp oil, or pumpkin
  seed oil

1 tbsp olive oil

1 tbsp lime juice

1 tbsp apple cider vinegar

2 tbsp snipped chives

sea salt and pepper

Hulled hemp seeds (or nuts) were a big surprise to me because I thought they'd be worthy but tasteless. Instead they tasted sweet and nutty, rather like crushed almonds. Keep in the fridge to preserve their goodness.

WHISK the dressing ingredients together in a bowl.

HALVE, stone, peel and roughly chop the avocados.

QUARTER, core and slice the apple.

TOSS the avocado and apple in the dressing.

ADD the sprouts, red onion and spinach and toss lightly.

SCATTER in the seeds and lightly toss again.

PILE onto a large platter and serve.

SCANDI
platter

SERVES 4

1 cucumber
½ tsp sea salt
1 tbsp caster sugar
2 tbsp white wine vinegar
2 tbsp chopped dill
300g peeled, cooked prawns
1 baby cos lettuce, washed
4 baby radishes, sliced
4 hard-boiled eggs, halved
50g salmon roe
crispbread to serve

This is a favourite, lazy, easy weekend lunch of mine, a sort of deconstructed Scandinavian smorgasbord. Serve with Scandinavian crispbread (eg Finn Crisp).

SLICE the cucumber lengthways, using a veggie peeler and avoiding the seeds.
TOSS the cucumber ribbons with the sea salt and half the sugar and leave for 20 minutes.
RINSE, drain and squeeze dry.
MIX the wine vinegar, remaining sugar and dill together.
ADD the prawns, toss well and leave for 10 minutes.
DRAIN the prawns and arrange on four platters.
ADD the pickled cucumber, cos leaves, radishes, eggs and salmon roe.
SERVE with crispbread.

WATERMELON
carpaccio

SERVES 4

4 rounds of watermelon,
  2cm thick
100g feta cheese
½ red onion, finely sliced
12 kalamata olives
½ tsp cracked black pepper
2 tbsp small oregano or basil
  leaves
2 tbsp extra virgin olive oil

This is the sort of cooling food I crave on a hot summer's day: juicy watermelon with Greek feta and olives. Add a drizzle of sweet-and-sour balsamic vinegar from a squeezy bottle, or a handful of rocket leaves.

CUT the rind from the watermelon slices.
ARRANGE on four dinner plates.
CRUMBLE the feta over the watermelon.
SCATTER with the red onion, olives and pepper.
STREW with the oregano.
DRIZZLE with the olive oil and eat.

ROAST CHICKEN,
walnut and tarragon salad

SERVES 4

500g pumpkin or butternut
 squash (with skin)
4 chicken quarters (leg and
 thigh)
olive oil to drizzle
2 tbsp walnut halves, toasted
1 frisée (curly endive)
2 tbsp tarragon leaves

DRESSING:

2 tbsp extra virgin olive oil
1 tbsp red wine vinegar
1 tsp Dijon mustard
1 tbsp white wine or water
sea salt and pepper

Roast chicken is one of the best dishes in the whole wide world, and this fast, light version turns it into a warm nutty salad. The frizzy curly endive gives it a soft, slightly bitter crunch.

HEAT the oven to 200°C/Gas 6.

CHOP the pumpkin roughly, discarding the seeds.

PLACE the chicken and pumpkin in a roasting tray.

DRIZZLE with olive oil, season well and bake for about 40 minutes until golden and tender.

ALLOW to cool slightly.

WARM the walnuts in the oven for 5 minutes.

WHISK the dressing ingredients together in a large bowl.

TEAR the chicken off the bone in large bite-sized pieces.

SEPARATE the frisée leaves and tear roughly.

TOSS the warm chicken, pumpkin, frisée and tarragon in the dressing.

DIVIDE among four dinner plates.

SCATTER with warm walnuts and eat.

RADICCHIO, BEETROOT
and grapefruit salad

SERVES 4

4 slices pancetta
8 baby beetroot or 4 medium
  beetroot, cooked
2 radicchio
1 pink grapefruit
handful of rocket leaves

DRESSING:

2 tbsp extra virgin olive oil
1 tbsp red wine vinegar
sea salt and pepper
1 tsp pink peppercorns

We need salads even more in winter, as a contrast to heavier dishes. Serve this one as a first course, or with grilled oil-rich fish like mackerel or salmon.

HEAT the grill.

LAY the pancetta slices on a foil-lined grill tray and grill until crisp.

HALVE or quarter the beetroot.

STRIP the leaves from the radicchio, wash well and cut into 1cm strips.

CUT the skin and pith away from the grapefruit.

PULL the segments apart, saving the juice.

WHISK the dressing ingredients together, adding a little grapefruit juice to taste.

TOSS the radicchio and rocket in the dressing and pile onto plates.

ADD the beetroot and grapefruit to any dressing left in the bowl, toss lightly and strew over the leaves.

CRUMBLE the crisp pancetta over the top and serve.

GLASS NOODLES
with chicken and prawns

SERVES 4

200g bean thread (glass) noodles
½ cucumber
10 cherry tomatoes
3 small red shallots, finely sliced
1 small red chilli, finely sliced
2 cooked chicken legs or breasts
8 cooked prawns, peeled
100g bean sprouts, rinsed
handful of mint, basil or
  coriander leaves
2 tbsp peanuts, roughly chopped
1 lime, quartered

DRESSING:

2 tbsp lime juice
2 tbsp Thai fish sauce
2 tbsp sweet chilli sauce
1 tbsp olive oil
1 tbsp sugar

This tangy noodle salad is so inviting it almost jumps up off the plate into your mouth. It's highly adjustable – drop the chicken or prawns if they don't suit – and great for lunchboxes and picnics.

PUT the noodles in a bowl, pour on boiling water to cover and leave for 4 minutes.

PEEL and finely slice the cucumber.

CUT the cherry tomatoes into quarters.

DRAIN the noodles and snip in half with scissors.

WHISK the dressing ingredients together in a large bowl.

ADD the tomatoes, cucumber, shallots and chilli, and toss gently.

SLICE the chicken against the grain.

TOSS lightly with the prawns, noodles, bean sprouts and herb leaves.

SCATTER with peanuts.

SERVE with lime wedges for squeezing.

PANZANELLA
with toasted almonds

SERVES 4

3 or 4 thick (2cm) slices day-old
   sourdough bread
virgin olive oil for brushing
½ cucumber
10 cherry tomatoes
4 ripe tomatoes
½ red onion, finely sliced
2 tbsp blanched whole almonds,
   toasted
2 tbsp Spanish green olives
2 tbsp basil leaves, torn

DRESSING:

3 tbsp extra virgin olive oil
2 tbsp red wine vinegar
sea salt and pepper

I feel sorry for people who treat bread as the enemy. The only enemy is bad food – not great-tasting, naturally leavened, low-GI sourdough bread that gives a rustic Italian salad like this real presence and character.

HEAT the grill.
BRUSH the bread with olive oil and grill on both sides.
CUT into 2cm cubes.
PEEL the cucumber, quarter lengthways and thickly slice.
HALVE the cherry tomatoes.
CHOP the other tomatoes roughly, catching the juices.
TOSS the bread, cucumber, tomatoes and their juices, onion, almonds, olives and basil in a large bowl.
WHISK the dressing ingredients together.
POUR over the salad, tossing gently with your hands.
STREW on a large platter and eat.

Raw food is food as nature intended – fresh, natural and full of antioxidants and enzymes. If your body is not used to digesting raw food, start gently with a refreshing **YOGHURT AND CUCUMBER SOUP:** in a blender, whiz 1 peeled, diced, deseeded cucumber with 1 litre natural low-fat yoghurt, 500ml iced water, 2 tbsp finely chopped dill, 1 crushed garlic clove, sea salt and pepper until smooth. Freeze for 2 hours until thick, then whiz again until it is smooth and frothy. Serve in chilled bowls or glasses as a light, summery appetiser. For 4.

This very chic **NICOISE CARPACCIO** fits with my belief that good food should also be good for you. The key is what you buy – it must be the freshest 'sashimi-grade' fish from a trusted supplier. Take 400g fresh tuna or salmon fillet and refrigerate to firm up. Using a very sharp knife, cut into paper-thin slices. Overlap on 4 plates and top each with a hard-boiled quail egg, green beans, cherry tomato, black olive, 2 slices of cooked potato, basil leaves and a curl of anchovy fillet. Drizzle with extra virgin olive oil and season with sea salt and pepper. For 4.

RAW X4

Sometimes, an ingredient is so perfect in its natural state, it's a shame to change it by cooking. I couldn't live on a diet of raw food, but I love a spicy **RAW SLAW** occasionally. Coarsely grate 300g peeled beetroot (wearing gloves) and finely shred 200g red cabbage. Whisk together 1 tsp Dijon mustard, 1 tbsp red wine vinegar, 2 tbsp extra virgin olive oil, 1 tsp poppy seeds, 1 tsp caster sugar, 1 tsp ground ginger, 1/2 tsp ground coriander, 1/2 tsp ground cumin, sea salt and pepper. Toss with the beetroot and cabbage, and chill. Top with a plop of yoghurt and scatter with poppy seeds to serve. For 4.

Crudos and ceviches aren't strictly raw but are 'cooked' by a natural citric acid, as in this fresh-tasting **SCALLOP AND LIME CRUDO:** clean four sublimely fresh large scallops, remove any coral, then finely slice into discs. For the dressing, toss a finely sliced shallot with 2 tbsp lime juice, 1 tsp pink peppercorns, 1 tsp caster sugar and sea salt. Arrange the scallop slices in a single layer on a large plate, top with the dressing and drizzle with a little extra virgin olive oil. Scatter with coriander and mint leaves to serve. It tastes so fresh, you'll wonder why we bother cooking anything at all. For 4.

The best thing about cooking soup is the wonderful smell. It's worth leaving the house while it simmers away on the hob – just so you can come back in the door hungry and breathe it all in, knowing you are about to be fed.

I used to think of soups as slow food, and let them simmer for hours, but now the sort of soups I like best are cooked pretty fast, before everything gets tired, including me. Slow cooking is good for getting the goodness out of bones and tough old vegetables, but if you use fresh ingredients, you don't want to cook all the freshness and nutrients out of them.

For the same reason, you want to eat soup soon after cooking rather than days later. Lots of recipes call for leaving the soup overnight, but I think that's only relevant when it is meat-based, so that any fat has a chance to rise to the surface and be skimmed off. If you want to make soup ahead, don't overcook it. Cool it quickly and freeze to have at a later date.

One of the best ways to lighten up your soups without any loss of flavour is to use vegetable stocks instead of meat-based stocks. You can easily make your own (see page 213), or buy a very respectable product called Marigold Organic Swiss bouillon powder, which smells invitingly of fresh carrot tops.

Another handy product is a good organic tomato juice, which I use as an instant vegetable stock for tomato-based soups and stews. It lightens, brightens and adds flavour where you might have just added water. And don't forget you can always turn your favourite stew or casserole into a soup by adding more liquid. It will taste lighter, go further and, because you're eating from a bowl, you won't automatically feel the need for potatoes on the side.

Most of the soups I really love qualify as meals in themselves, like spicy Indian lentil soups (dal), or tangy, herby bowls of soupy noodles.

Soupy food is also my first thought for supper if I've had lunch out. Two big meals a day makes me feel uncomfortably full, but soup sits lightly on the stomach at night, while still giving me a 'proper' meal and great flavour and goodness.

If you are planning on an early night, soup is the best evening meal you can have, so you won't have to go to bed on a full stomach. Soup is also useful when you are eating out, as it is lighter and leaner than so many other first courses (interrogate your waiter as to the presence of excess cream). It's a good option for a working lunch too, being easier to digest than a heavy sandwich – and all that broth leaves you feeling very satisfied.

CHICKEN TORTILLA
soup with avocado

SERVES 4

2 tbsp olive oil

1 onion, halved and finely sliced

4 garlic cloves, finely sliced

4 tomatoes, chopped

1.2 litres chicken or vegetable
  stock

1 tsp ground cumin

2 tbsp tomato purée (paste)

½ tsp sea salt

½ tsp sugar

1 mild green chilli, sliced

1 chicken breast, skinned and
  boned

1 avocado, peeled and sliced

1 small red onion, finely sliced

handful of coriander leaves

handful of corn chips

1 lime, quartered

A lot of Tex-Mex food is heavy on calories and oily with cheese, but Mexico's regional food – like this Yucatan Peninsula *sopa de lima* – is much lighter and brighter. It's the sort of soup you could happily have every day.

HEAT the olive oil in a pan.

COOK the onion for 5 minutes.

ADD the garlic and tomatoes and cook for 5 minutes.

POUR in the stock.

ADD the cumin, tomato purée, sea salt, sugar and chilli and bring to the boil, stirring.

SLICE the chicken breast finely, add to the pan and simmer gently for 10 minutes until tender.

DIVIDE the hot soup among warm bowls.

TOP with the avocado, red onion and coriander.

BREAK up the corn chips and scatter over the soup.

SERVE with lime wedges for squeezing.

TUSCAN BEAN
soup

SERVES 4

600g cavolo nero (or other
leafy veg)
2 tbsp olive oil
2 celery stalks, finely sliced
1 leek, finely sliced
1 large carrot, finely chopped
400g potatoes, peeled and
finely diced
1 tsp tomato purée (paste)
4 thyme sprigs
2 bay leaves
1.5 litres boiling stock or water
400g canned white beans,
rinsed
sea salt and pepper
2 tbsp chopped parsley
extra virgin olive oil to drizzle

This is my favourite way of eating those all-important,
dark green leafy vegetables. Cavolo nero (Tuscan black
cabbage) is brilliant here, but curly kale, Swiss chard,
silver beet and Savoy cabbage all work a treat, too.

SHRED the cavolo nero (or other) leaves, discarding any
large stems.
HEAT the olive oil in a heavy-based saucepan.
COOK the celery, leek and carrot gently for 10 minutes.
ADD the cavolo nero, potatoes, tomato purée, thyme
and bay leaves.
POUR in the stock and simmer, covered, for 20 minutes
or until the vegetables are tender.
MASH one-third of the beans to a paste and stir into the
soup with the rest of the beans.
ADD sea salt and pepper to taste and heat through.
DIVIDE among warm bowls.
SCATTER with parsley.
DRIZZLE with extra virgin olive oil.

ZUPPA
di pesce

SERVES 4

2 tbsp olive oil
1 onion, halved and finely sliced
2 garlic cloves, finely sliced
2 bay leaves
500g tomatoes, canned or fresh
150ml dry white wine
pinch of dried chilli flakes
½ tsp paprika
sea salt and pepper
2 potatoes, peeled and quartered
1 tbsp tomato purée (paste)
500ml boiling stock or water
600g white fish fillets (eg hake,
    cod, whiting, gurnard, snapper)
8 prawns, peeled, tails left intact
2 tbsp oregano leaves
extra virgin olive oil to drizzle

There is soup, and then there is *zuppa*, a rustic Italian soup that is a meal in itself, traditionally served over a thick slice of garlicky bread. I skip the bread in this case, because there is so much else going on.

HEAT the olive oil in a large pan.

ADD the onion, garlic, bay leaves and tomatoes, and cook for 5 minutes.

STIR in the wine, chilli flakes, paprika, sea salt and pepper and bring to the boil.

ADD the potatoes, tomato purée and stock.

SIMMER for 30 minutes until the potatoes are tender.

CUT the fish into bite-sized chunks.

ADD to the soup with the prawns, and simmer gently for 5 minutes.

LADLE into warm, shallow bowls.

SCATTER with oregano.

DRIZZLE with a little extra virgin olive oil.

BRILLIANT
watercress soup

SERVES 4

2 tsp butter

1 onion, finely chopped

1 leek, finely sliced

2 garlic cloves, finely sliced

250g potatoes, peeled and diced

sea salt and pepper

freshly grated nutmeg

1.2 litres boiling light stock or
    water

200g spinach, well washed

200g watercress, well washed,
    plus sprigs to serve

4 tbsp natural low-fat yoghurt

The French use peppery, iron-rich watercress soup as an occasional weekend detox. It's packed with vitamins and minerals, and contains no cream or other excess fat. To get full value, serve it as soon as you've made it.

MELT the butter in a pan and cook the onion and leek for 5 minutes.

ADD the garlic, potatoes, sea salt, pepper and nutmeg.

POUR in the stock, stirring briskly.

SIMMER until the potatoes are soft, about 15 minutes.

DROP in the spinach, pushing it down until it wilts.

ADD the watercress, again pushing it into the soup until just wilted.

WHIZ in a blender until very smooth.

REHEAT gently and pour into warm bowls.

DRIZZLE with yoghurt and top with watercress sprigs.

ICED BEETROOT
soup

SERVES 6 TO 8

3 shallots

2 celery stalks

500g beetroot, cooked and
   peeled

2 garlic cloves, crushed

2 tbsp red wine vinegar

2 tbsp extra virgin olive oil

300ml vegetable stock or water

sea salt and pepper

1 tbsp horseradish cream

100g thick Greek yoghurt

chives to finish

Chilled soup needs a lot of flavour to be as tempting as hot soup, but this one makes the grade; being spicy, earthy, sweet and sharp all at once. Serve in small bowls or glasses for the drama queen effect.

CHOP the shallots, celery and beetroot finely.

MIX with the crushed garlic, wine vinegar and olive oil.

COVER and marinate for 2 hours or overnight.

WHIZ to a smooth purée in a blender.

ADD the stock, sea salt and pepper, and whiz.

CHILL until ready to serve.

POUR into 6 or 8 chilled small glasses.

STIR the horseradish cream with the yoghurt.

PLOP on top of each soup.

GRIND over some pepper.

SPEAR with a chive.

SPRING
minestrone

SERVES 4

2 tbsp extra virgin olive oil

2 leeks, finely sliced

2 celery stalks, finely sliced

1.2 litres boiling chicken or
vegetable stock

8 baby carrots, peeled

100g small soup pasta, such
as stelline (stars)

1 green courgette (zucchini),
finely sliced

1 yellow courgette (zucchini),
finely sliced

100g shelled peas

2 pink radishes, finely sliced

sea salt and pepper

2 tbsp pesto

Light and fragrant, this springtime minestrone gathers up all the bright and beautiful colours of baby spring vegetables. Adding boiling hot stock to the vegetables in the pan really captures their sweetness.

HEAT the olive oil in a saucepan.

ADD the leeks and celery and cook until soft.

POUR in the hot stock and add the baby carrots.

SIMMER for 10 minutes.

COOK the pasta in boiling salted water until al dente.

DRAIN and add to the soup.

TOSS in the courgettes, peas and radishes.

SEASON with sea salt and pepper.

SIMMER for 3 minutes, keeping the colours bright.

LADLE into shallow pasta bowls.

ADD a plop of pesto and serve.

SUMO
soup

SERVES 4

1.5 litres chicken stock
½ daikon radish, sliced
2 leeks, thickly sliced
1 carrot, sliced
2 chicken breasts, skinned and
  boned
8 fresh shiitake or abalone
  mushrooms, sliced
2 baby pak choi, halved
  lengthways
200g udon noodles
60ml soy sauce
40ml mirin (sweet rice wine)
sea salt

This is a 'good luck' soup based on *chankonabe*, the daily fuel of Japanese sumo wrestlers. It won't turn you into a sumo wrestler, however, unless you eat ten huge bowls of it a day, washed down with plenty of beer.

BRING the stock to the boil in a saucepan.
ADD the sliced radish, leeks and carrot and simmer for 15 minutes until tender.
CUT the chicken into bite-sized slices and add to the pan with the mushrooms and pak choi.
SIMMER for 5 minutes, skimming if necessary.
COOK the udon noodles separately in boiling water for 8 minutes or until just tender, then drain.
DIVIDE the noodles among warm, deep soup bowls.
STIR the soy sauce and mirin into the soup and season with sea salt to taste.
LADLE the soup over the noodles and serve.

SPINACH
chana dal

SERVES 4

200g chana dal (yellow split
   pulse), rinsed
2 tbsp vegetable oil
1 onion, finely sliced
1 tbsp grated fresh ginger
1 tsp cumin seeds
200g canned chopped tomatoes
1 mild green chilli, sliced
½ tsp ground turmeric
½ tsp cayenne pepper
1 tsp ground coriander
1 tsp sea salt
1 tsp garam masala
400g spinach, well washed

I call this a soup because I like to keep my dal lightly soupy and spicy, rather than thick and heavy. You could live on it if you had to, or even if you didn't.

SOAK the dal in cold water for 30 minutes, then drain, rinse and tip into a large saucepan.

POUR in 1.2 litres water and bring to the boil, skimming. Simmer, partly covered, for 20 minutes.

HEAT the oil in a fry pan.

ADD the onion, ginger and cumin seeds and cook for 5 minutes.

STIR in the tomatoes, chilli, turmeric, cayenne, coriander and sea salt.

ADD the mix to the dal and simmer for 20 minutes, adding extra water if necessary.

WHISK in the garam masala.

ADD the spinach, pushing it down until wilted.

SPOON into warm bowls and serve.

FLOATING MARKET
fish soup

SERVES 4

600g white fish fillets (eg cod,
    whiting, gurnard, snapper)
sea salt and pepper
100g bean thread (glass) noodles
2 lemongrass stalks
1.2 litres chicken stock
3 shallots, finely sliced
1 mild red chilli, sliced
2 tbsp tamarind purée
2 tbsp Thai fish sauce
1 tbsp sugar
100g bean sprouts, washed
2 tomatoes, chopped
small handful of Asian basil
    and/or coriander leaves
1 lime, quartered

I love this soup. It's such delicious proof that you can lighten up your cooking and eating without losing out on flavour and freshness. I especially love it on those 'my body is a temple' nights when I'm not drinking, as it makes me feel I'm not missing out on a thing.

CUT the fish into bite-sized chunks and toss with sea salt and pepper.

PUT the noodles in a bowl, pour on boiling water to cover and leave for 4 minutes, then drain.

TRIM the lemongrass to its inner, tender white part and finely slice.

PUT the stock, shallots, chilli, tamarind and lemongrass in a saucepan and bring to the boil.

SIMMER for 10 minutes.

STIR in the fish sauce, sugar and chunks of fish.

SIMMER for 5 minutes.

ADD the bean sprouts, noodles and tomatoes.

SIMMER for 1 minute until hot.

DIVIDE among warm bowls.

SCATTER with basil and/or coriander.

SERVE with lime wedges for squeezing.

Good bread is good for you. So choose real bread that is slow to eat and slow to digest – like low-GI pumpernickel, rye, pain levain, sourdough, wholemeal – and get slow and steady energy as well. But instead of having it on the side, make it the base plate of your meal. For an instant **SALMON SMORREBROD:** finely chop 100g fresh salmon fillet and 100g smoked salmon. Toss with a dash of lemon juice, 1 tbsp chopped dill, sea salt and pepper. Lightly spread on two slices of plain or toasted pumpernickel or dark rye bread and top with hard-boiled egg and chopped dill. For 2.

A ploughman's lunch in a British pub used to mean just bread and cheese. But it's far more interesting with rare roast beef and mustard as well. So go for a **PLOUGHMAN'S:** spread 2 slices of pumpernickel or dark rye bread with mustard. Top with slices of rare roast beef from the deli counter or last night's roast dinner, a little aged Cheddar cheese, crumbly Lancashire or tangy Stilton, and a thick slice or two of pickled onion. Scatter with sea salt and pepper, serve with a cold ale and you'll have plenty of energy to help you plough through the rest of the day. For 2.

BREAD X4

If you don't eat avocado for its oleic acid to protect your heart, then at least eat it for its vitamin E, which is good for your skin. I have this spicy avocado-on-rye for breakfast whenever I am holidaying by the beach. For me, its just like **SUNSHINE ON TOAST:** Peel and stone a firm, ripe avocado and crush or dice. Spread over 2 slices of pumpernickel or dark rye bread. Top with sliced tomato and sliced pickled jalapeño chillies. Drizzle with lime juice, avocado oil (a revelation) or green (jalapeño) Tabasco sauce, and scatter with sea salt and pepper. For 2.

This is one of the great raw dishes of the world, and one of the pleasures of a Parisian lunch. For **STEAK TARTARE:** you will need 100g very fresh beef fillet, 1 anchovy fillet, 2 gherkins and 1 tsp rinsed salted capers. Very finely chop by hand or whiz in a food processor, adding 1 tsp Dijon mustard, a dash of Tabasco and a dash of Worcestershire sauce. Spread the tartare on two slices of plain or toasted dark rye or pumpernickel bread. Top with a fresh egg yolk, still in its half shell, so you can add a little egg to the meat as you eat it, enriching and binding it. For 2.

There is no excuse for eating bland, boring food, when there are so many different spices and chillies in the world.

I'm not thinking of cheap thrills – anyone can sprinkle coarse chilli powder over food and bring tears to the eyes. I'm talking about how to use the spices, chillies and pastes we have in our cupboard to make our food taste more exciting, and to save us from having to add excessive amounts of fat, salts and sugars to get our kicks.

Spices can add sweetness, warmth and bite, changing our food before our eyes. They make everything taste different. I eat a lot of fish, for instance, which could get a bit repetitive, so I try to make it quite different every time – dusting it with paprika one night, coating it with curry paste the next, or serving it with spiced-up couscous.

The bigger the variety of foods and flavours we eat, the better off we are and the less bored we become. I've noticed that when I am bored, I keep eating, because I don't feel satisfied. But when I can really taste every mouthful, I don't seem to eat more than I need.

Spices also make it more interesting to eat bland-but-good-for-you foods like tofu, pulses and lentils. They make your food glow, without changing the natural flavour of the main ingredients. In fact, they boost it, rather than bury it.

It's not just what they do for our food, it's what they do for us. Coriander and cumin are said to be good for the digestion, turmeric improves liver function and skin tone, ginger and black pepper help prevent coughs and colds, and nutmeg is meant to relieve stress, although I have yet to see the benefits of that myself.

It's also important to update your spices every year, so they don't sit there getting stale and dull. Upgrade your chilli options, too, by ditching the cheap cayenne and getting the right heat for the job. That could mean fresh red chillies, dried roasted red chilli flakes from Chinatown, or single-variety dried Mexican chillies such as fruity ancho or smoky chipotle. I'm also a big fan of Tabasco sauce, pickled jalapeño chillies, Japanese togarashi pepper, Thai sweet chilli sauce and North African harissa.

I very rarely deseed chillies, because the capsaicin, the alkaloid that gives chilli its burn, is not so much in the seeds as in the membrane around the seeds. If you do want to disarm a chilli, however, just chop off either end and shove a chopstick right through the middle, pushing out the seeds and membrane. And if you're not sure how hot a fresh chilli is, add it to your cooking thickly sliced, rather than finely chopped. That way, you have more of a chance of either avoiding it, or finding it.

SOM TUM
rice paper rolls

SERVES 4

300g green (unripened) papaya or mango
1 cucumber
2 red shallots, finely sliced
1 mild red chilli, finely sliced
1 tbsp caster sugar
20 cherry tomatoes, quartered
3 tbsp mint or basil leaves, torn, plus extra to serve
2 tbsp lime juice
2 tbsp Thai fish sauce
6 x 20cm dried rice paper rounds

TO SERVE:

4 tbsp sweet, seedy, chilli sauce
2 tbsp roasted cashews, crushed

Wrap Thai green papaya salad (*som tum*) in Vietnamese rice paper (*bahn trang*) for a tangy, fresh, crunchy, hot, sweet and sour experience. Serve as a first course, a lunch, or anytime with a drink.

PEEL the green papaya and cucumber.
SLICE the flesh lengthways, using a veggie peeler.
CUT each slice into thin matchstick strips.
POUND the shallots, chilli, sugar and half the tomatoes to a rough paste.
TOSS with the remaining tomatoes, mint, green papaya and cucumber.
ADD lime juice and fish sauce and adjust to taste.
MULCH and squelch the salad with your hands.
DIP each rice paper into hot water and lay on a surface.
PICK up a small handful of salad and squeeze it dry.
PLACE on a paper round and roll up, tucking in the ends.
REPEAT with the rest.
CUT in half and scatter with mint leaves.
SERVE with sweet chilli sauce and cashews for dipping.

SPICE-GRILLED
mackerel

SERVES 4

4 mackerel, about 300g each
2 tbsp Thai red curry paste
1 tsp sugar
sea salt and pepper
2 tbsp coconut milk
1 cucumber, peeled
12 cherry tomatoes, halved
2 tbsp mint leaves
dash of Thai fish sauce
dash of lime juice
1 lime, quartered

You don't have to mollycoddle fish like mackerel – they're so rich and oily they can take whatever you throw at them. So slash them, coat them in red curry paste and coconut milk, then throw them on the grill.

RINSE the fish and pat dry.
SLASH the thickest part of the flesh on both sides several times.
MIX the curry paste with the sugar, sea salt, pepper and coconut milk.
SPREAD half the curry mix over one side of the fish.
GRILL for 5 minutes, then coat the other side with curry paste.
TURN the fish and grill for 10 minutes or until the skin starts to crackle and the fish is cooked.
SLICE the cucumber finely.
TOSS with the tomatoes, mint, fish sauce and lime juice.
SERVE the grilled mackerel with the cucumber salad and lime wedges.

SPICY OKRA
curry

SERVES 4

1 tbsp vegetable oil

1 onion, halved and finely sliced

1 tsp cumin seeds

1 red or green chilli, finely sliced

400g canned tomatoes

1 tbsp tomato purée (paste)

1 tsp fennel seeds

1 tsp ground coriander

½ tsp turmeric

½ tsp sea salt

1 tsp sugar

400g small okra, washed and
  carefully trimmed

1 tsp nigella seeds

2 tbsp coriander leaves

Okra is an extraordinary vegetable, with a lovely grassy flavour. Buy small ones and leave whole – don't chop or cut into them, unless you want a sticky, gloopy mess. Serve with rice or flat bread, or grilled meat or fish.

HEAT the oil in a pan and add the onion, cumin seeds and chilli.

COOK for 5 minutes or until the onion has softened.

ADD the tomatoes with their juice, tomato purée, fennel seeds, ground coriander, turmeric, sea salt and sugar.

POUR in 125ml water, stirring.

ADD the okra and simmer for 20 minutes or until tender.

SCATTER nigella seeds and coriander leaves over the curry and serve.

SPICED
cevapcici

SERVES 4 / MAKES 16

500g minced beef
250g minced lamb or pork
2 garlic cloves, crushed
pinch of allspice or nutmeg
pinch of ground cloves
1 tsp paprika
good pinch of cayenne pepper
1 tsp sea salt
¼ tsp pepper
1 tbsp olive oil
1 small onion, finely sliced
1 lemon, quartered

If you make your own sausages, you know exactly what is in them, and what isn't. Spiced cevapcici (pronounced 'chevapcheechee') are made without eggs, flour, bread, additives, preservatives or skins. Serve with ajvar, a spicy aubergine and red pepper relish (page 214).

MIX the beef and lamb in a bowl with the garlic, allspice, cloves, paprika, cayenne, sea salt and pepper.
MULCH well with your hands.
WET your hands with cold water.
FORM the mixture into small, flattened sausage shapes, about 8cm long.
HEAT the grill or barbecue.
BRUSH the sausages with olive oil.
GRILL or barbecue, turning once after 5 minutes, until well browned on both sides.
SCATTER the onion over the sausages.
SERVE with lemon wedges for squeezing.

THAI MUSSELS
with sweet potato

SERVES 4

750g orange-fleshed sweet
  potatoes, peeled
sea salt
1.5kg fresh live mussels
2 tbsp vegetable oil
3 shallots, finely sliced
3 garlic cloves, finely sliced
1 red chilli, finely sliced
2 tbsp Thai fish sauce
3 tbsp sweet, seedy chilli sauce
1 tbsp sugar
handful of basil, torn
handful of mint, torn
handful of coriander, torn
2 tbsp lime juice
1 extra lime, cut into wedges

Hot, sweet, sour and spicy, this is a great dish to share with a few friends, along with a big bowl of rice and a cold beer or two.

CUT the sweet potatoes into large bite-sized chunks.

COOK in simmering salted water for 15 minutes until tender, then drain.

SCRUB the mussels, pull out the beards and discard any that don't close when sharply tapped.

HEAT the oil, 250ml water, the shallots, garlic and chilli in a lidded heavy-based pan and bring to the boil.

THROW in the mussels, cover tightly and cook for a minute or two, then give the pan a good shake.

LIFT out any opened mussels with tongs and set aside.

COVER again and repeat, discarding any mussels that don't open.

ADD the sweet potatoes, fish sauce, chilli sauce and sugar to the broth and heat through, stirring.

ADD the mussels, herbs and lime juice, tossing well.

SERVE at once, with lime wedges and steamed rice.

SINGAPORE CHILLI
prawns

SERVES 4

5cm knob of fresh ginger
2 tbsp vegetable oil
2 garlic cloves, finely sliced
2 red chillies, finely sliced
16 raw prawns (about 1kg)
2 tbsp sweet chilli sauce
4 tbsp tomato ketchup
250ml hot chicken stock
½ tsp sea salt
2 tsp sugar
2 tsp cornflour
2 tbsp coriander leaves
1 lime, quartered

This is the same rich, hot, gingery, garlicky sauce used in the famous Singaporean chilli crab. Leave the prawns in their shells – much more messy, but much more fun.

CUT the ginger into matchsticks.
HEAT a wok, then add the oil.
TOSS in the ginger, garlic and chillies, and fry, stirring, for 30 seconds.
ADD the prawns and stir-fry over high heat for 1 minute, tossing well.
ADD the chilli sauce, ketchup, stock, sea salt and sugar.
BRING to the boil, stirring, and simmer for 2 minutes.
MIX the cornflour with 2 tbsp cold water to a paste.
ADD to the pan and stir until the sauce thickens.
SCATTER with coriander and lime wedges.
SERVE with rice or noodles.

KICKASS CHILLI
bean tacos

SERVES 4

800g canned red kidney beans

4 tbsp olive oil

1 onion, finely chopped

2 garlic cloves, crushed

pinch of cayenne pepper

2 tsp cumin seeds, freshly ground

sea salt and pepper

8 taco shells

3 tomatoes, finely chopped

1 sweet green pepper (capsicum),
   deseeded and finely chopped

1 tbsp lime juice

2 tbsp chopped coriander leaves

1 cos or romaine lettuce, finely
   shredded

pickled jalapeño chillies to serve

Tacos don't have to be heavy and cheesy. Try stuffing them with chilli-spiced beans, crisp lettuce and a fresh salsa instead, and feed to the hungry hordes.

HEAT the oven to 180°C/Gas 4.

DRAIN the kidney beans, rinse and drain again.

HEAT 2 tbsp olive oil in a fry pan.

COOK the onion for 10 minutes until soft.

ADD the kidney beans, garlic, cayenne, cumin, sea salt and pepper.

POUR in 300ml water and simmer for 10 minutes.

MASH the beans roughly in the pan using a potato masher and set aside.

HEAT the taco shells in the oven for 3 minutes while you make the salsa.

TOSS the tomatoes, green pepper, lime juice, coriander, sea salt and pepper with remaining olive oil.

FILL the taco shells with lettuce, beans and salsa.

TOP with jalapeño chillies and serve.

SPICED YOGHURT
chicken

SERVES 4

200g natural low-fat yoghurt

2 tbsp lemon juice

2 garlic cloves, crushed

1 tbsp finely grated fresh ginger

1 small green chilli, finely sliced

2 tsp garam masala

1 tsp paprika

1 tsp turmeric

pinch of cayenne pepper

½ tsp sea salt

1 tbsp vegetable oil

4 chicken breasts, skinned

2 tbsp coriander leaves

LEMON YOGHURT:

1 tbsp preserved (salted)
   lemons, rinsed

100g natural low-fat yoghurt

Yoghurt makes a good, quick marinade because it not only tenderises the chicken, it carries the spices into it as well. Serve with lemon-scented rice.

COMBINE the yoghurt, lemon juice, garlic, ginger, chilli, spices, sea salt and oil in a non-reactive bowl; mix well.

CUT a few slashes in the thicker part of the chicken.

COAT the chicken in the marinade and leave for about 30 minutes.

HEAT the oven to 200°C/Gas 6.

PLACE the chicken on a rack over a foil-lined baking tray.

BAKE for 30 minutes or until golden.

DICE the preserved lemons and mix with the yoghurt.

PLACE the chicken on warm plates.

SCATTER with coriander.

SERVE with the lemon yoghurt and steamed rice.

CHICKEN SATAY
with cucumber

SERVES 4

500g chicken breasts, skinless
3 tbsp soy sauce
1 tbsp vegetable oil
1 tbsp lime juice
1 tsp ground cumin
1 tsp ground coriander
pinch of cayenne pepper
2 garlic cloves, crushed
sea salt
1 cucumber
1 lime or lemon, quartered

PEANUT SAUCE:

1 tbsp oyster sauce
1 tbsp crunchy peanut butter
3 tbsp sweet chilli sauce
lime juice to taste

Throw these skewers on the barbecue and the sweet, spicy smoke will make everyone ravenously hungry. Serve with cooling cucumber and bowls of spicy peanut sauce for dipping.

SOAK 16 bamboo skewers in water to prevent burning.
CUT the chicken into 16 slices, about 1cm wide.
LAY on a board and cover with plastic.
BASH lightly, to flatten.
MIX the soy with the oil, lime juice, ground spices, garlic and sea salt.
COAT the chicken in the spicy marinade and leave for 30 minutes.
SLICE the cucumber lengthways, using a veggie peeler.
MIX the peanut sauce ingredients together in a bowl.
HEAT up the grill or barbecue.
THREAD the chicken onto the skewers.
GRILL or barbecue for 2 minutes on each side.
SERVE with the cucumber, peanut sauce and lime wedges for squeezing.

TOGARASHI
oven chips

SERVES 4 AS A SIDE DISH

2 huge baking potatoes (250g
   each) or 4 large ones
2 tbsp olive oil
1 tsp sea salt flakes
1 tsp caster sugar
½ tsp black pepper
1 tsp togarashi pepper

These are baked, not fried, for those times you really feel like chips. Togarashi is a Japanese sprinkle made of dried chilli, sansho pepper, sesame seeds and ground seaweed, which makes potatoes far more exciting.

HEAT the oven to 220°C/Gas 7.

TRIM the ends off the potatoes and cut lengthways into long chips (9 or 12 if huge, 4 to 6 if smaller).

TOSS with olive oil to coat.

ARRANGE in a single layer on a lightly oiled baking tray.

BAKE for 40 minutes until golden and tender.

CRUSH the sea salt, sugar and peppers to a powder.

TOSS the potatoes in half the togarashi mix, saving the rest for another great potato chip moment.

SERVE with simple grills, roast chicken, pan-fried fish or home-made burgers.

You can live without meat, but you can't live without flavour. If you're 100% vegetarian, or even 60 to 70% like so many of us, then your food needs to be stacked with flavour and excitement. It's really not that difficult.

Vegetarian food isn't just good food with the meat taken out, but great food that provides sources of protein other than meat. So it's still all about fresh and seasonal produce, piquant relishes, time-saving sauces and modern ideas – with the protein coming from things like cheese, tofu, lentils, pulses, eggs (not for vegans) and nuts. That means using soy sauce instead of fish sauce, capers rather than anchovies, sun-dried tomatoes instead of prosciutto and aubergine and mushrooms in place of meat.

As for any cooking, it's the little things that can make a big difference: fresh, mild cheeses to melt over pizzas and bread, fresh herbs, aromatic spices, garlic, chilli, lemon, lime, sea salt and freshly milled black pepper. From Asia, miso (fermented soybean paste), mirin (sweet rice wine) and hoisin sauce add richness. From the Mediterranean, clever pestos and tapenades are instant flavour hits.

One thing I sometimes find missing in meat-free meals is a textural crispness or crunch, so I often add freshly toasted nuts to salads and rice and vegetable dishes, or bake little parmesan crisps (page 140) to serve on the side of soups.

At home, I don't differentiate between meat and meat-free meals; it's all just good food I crave in different seasons – like soft, oozing polenta topped with mushrooms; spicy Indian curries of meaty aubergine; or grilled Mediterranean vegetables stacked with melting mozzarella.

I'm not a big fan of chasing the latest superfood fad, but leafy green vegetables are real superheroes, and they're probably the most powerful anti-cancer friends we have. Eat lightly cooked broccoli, spinach, kale, Swiss chard, pea sprouts tossed in garlicky olive oil, and you can feel actually them doing you good.

The fresher your vegetables, the more good they will do you, which is why properly snap-frozen vegetables can contain more nutrients than 'fresh' ones that are days old. Don't chop or process your vegetables too much, and don't cook them too long. Try to retain their natural shapes and colours in the cooking (think how beautiful asparagus is when it's still a brilliant green), and you will enjoy them so much more – and have a balanced diet without even trying.

Turn to Extras (pages 212–5) for a few good, simple basics like vegetable broths and relishes – and you'll find meat-free recipes in every chapter, not just this one.

JAPANESE MUSHROOM
noodles

SERVES 4

4 dried shiitake mushrooms

250g dried udon noodles

200g fresh Japanese mushrooms

2 tbsp vegetable oil

1 tbsp finely shredded fresh ginger

sea salt and pepper

1 tbsp miso paste

1 tbsp mirin (sweet rice wine)

2 tbsp soy sauce

chives or spring (green) onion
    tops to finish

Japanese mushrooms always remind me of the intricate art of origami, with their wonderfully weird shapes and textures. Use any combination you like – shimeji, oyster, shiitake, enoki or nameko.

SOAK the dried mushrooms in 250ml boiling water for 30 minutes, then drain, reserving the water.

SLICE the caps finely, discarding the stalks.

COOK the udon noodles in simmering salted water for 8 minutes until tender, then drain.

TRIM the fresh mushrooms and slice thickly.

HEAT the oil in a fry pan.

ADD the ginger and fresh and dried mushrooms.

COOK gently for 3 minutes or until soft.

STIR in the mushroom water, sea salt and pepper, and simmer for 3 minutes.

PUT the miso paste in a small bowl and whisk in 3 tbsp of the hot stock.

ADD the miso, mirin and soy to the mushrooms.

TOSS with the drained noodles.

SERVE in warm bowls scattered with chives.

MIXED GRILL
with mozzarella

SERVES 4

2 medium aubergines (eggplant)
2 red peppers
olive oil for brushing
2 balls of fresh mozzarella
2 tbsp basil or parsley leaves
sea salt and pepper
1 tsp basil pesto
2 tbsp extra virgin olive oil

I never fry aubergine slices, because they absorb so much oil in the pan it's like eating a sponge. Lightly oiled and grilled, however, they go crisp and nutty – perfect to 'sandwich' melting mozzarella and grilled peppers.

HEAT the grill.

SLICE each aubergine crossways into 4 thick rounds, discarding the ends.

CUT the 4 'walls' from each red pepper, discarding the core and seeds.

BRUSH the aubergine and red pepper slices with olive oil.

GRILL on both sides until tender.

DRAIN the mozzarella and cut into 8 slices.

STACK a slice of mozzarella and red pepper on each aubergine slice.

HEAT under the grill for 1 minute.

PLACE 4 stacks on top of the other 4 stacks.

SCATTER with basil, sea salt and pepper.

MIX the pesto with the extra virgin olive oil.

DRIZZLE the stacks with pesto oil and serve.

ROAST VEGETABLES
with garlic and chilli

SERVES 4

500g butternut squash
500g waxy potatoes, scrubbed
2 parsnips, peeled
6 baby carrots, peeled
2 heads of garlic, halved
   crossways
4 rosemary sprigs, plus extra to
   serve
4 red chillies, halved lengthways
2 tbsp extra virgin olive oil
½ tsp black pepper
4 plum tomatoes

DRESSING:

1 tbsp balsamic vinegar
2 tbsp extra virgin olive oil
1 tsp Dijon mustard
sea salt and pepper

I used to cook a huge roast meal once a week, until I realised it was the roast veggies I craved, not the meat. Now, this is the roast I have when I'm not having a roast – spiced up with lots of garlic, chilli and rosemary.

HEAT the oven to 220°C/Gas 7.
CUT the squash into wedges, discarding any seeds.
HALVE the potatoes and parsnips lengthways.
PLACE in a roasting tray with the squash and carrots.
ADD the garlic, rosemary, chillies, olive oil and pepper.
TOSS well, then bake for 30 minutes.
ADD the tomatoes to the pan and toss again.
BAKE for 30 minutes, shaking the pan occasionally.
PILE onto warm plates and season well.
TUCK in a few fresh rosemary sprigs.
WHISK the dressing ingredients together.
DRIZZLE over the vegetables and serve.

SWEETCORN RISOTTO
with chives

SERVES 4

4 fresh corn cobs
1 onion, quartered
1 tbsp olive oil
15g butter, plus a small knob
1 onion, finely chopped
350g arborio or other risotto rice
150ml dry white wine
1 tbsp finely snipped chives
sea salt and pepper
2 tbsp freshly grated parmesan

This is clever – you make the sweet, nutty broth from the stripped corn cobs, while their kernels add colour and freshness.

STRIP the husks and threads from the corn cobs.
SHEAR off the kernels with a sharp knife.
SIMMER the cobs and quartered onion in 1.5 litres salted water for 30 minutes.
STRAIN the broth and return to the pan.
ADD the corn kernels and simmer for 5 minutes.
STRAIN the broth, reserving the corn.
HEAT the olive oil and knob of butter in a medium pan.
COOK the chopped onion until softened.
TIP in the rice, stirring well with a wooden spoon.
STIR in the wine, letting it bubble away for 1 minute.
ADD the broth, a ladleful at a time, stirring well until the rice is tender and creamy.
ADD the corn kernels, chives, butter, sea salt, pepper and parmesan.
HEAT through and serve.

CHILLI BEAN
tofu

SERVES 4

1 large aubergine (eggplant)
500g fresh tofu
2cm knob of fresh ginger
2 tbsp vegetable oil
2 garlic cloves, finely sliced
2 tbsp hot chilli bean sauce
1 tsp sugar
1 tbsp Chinese rice wine or
  dry sherry
2 tbsp soy sauce
2 spring (green) onions,
  chopped

My veggo version of the famous *ma po* beancurd is just as hearty, spicy and satisfying as the original. Add a pinch of Sichuan pepper for a real kick.

HEAT the oven to 180°C/Gas 4.
PRICK the aubergine well and bake for 40 minutes.
COOL and chop into 1cm dice.
DRAIN the tofu and cut into 2cm dice.
CUT the ginger into matchsticks.
HEAT the wok, then add the oil.
COOK the garlic and ginger, stirring, for 1 minute.
ADD the aubergine, chilli sauce, sugar, rice wine and soy.
STIR in 150ml water and simmer for 10 minutes.
ADD the tofu and simmer for 5 minutes or until the sauce thickens.
SCATTER with spring onions and serve.

WHITE BEAN
polpettine

SERVES 2

400g canned white beans
40g parmesan, freshly grated
2 tbsp chopped parsley
sea salt and pepper
freshly grated nutmeg
½ egg, beaten
2 tbsp dried breadcrumbs, plus
  extra for coating
1 tbsp olive oil
500g spinach, well washed
extra virgin olive oil to drizzle
1 lemon, quartered

These are like flat 'meatballs' – made with white beans and parmesan instead of meat. Serve with wilted spinach and a spicy tomato salsa, or make smaller fritters and serve them with drinks.

DRAIN the beans, rinse and mash roughly.

MIX with the parmesan, parsley, sea salt, pepper and nutmeg to taste.

BEAT in the egg.

MIX in the breadcrumbs gradually, until the mixture is firm enough to mould.

SHAPE into 4 patties and lightly coat in breadcrumbs.

HEAT the olive oil in a non-stick fry pan.

COOK the patties gently on both sides until golden.

HEAT a dry fry pan, add the spinach and toss well over high heat until wilted.

DRAIN and toss in a little extra virgin olive oil.

SERVE the patties with the spinach and lemon wedges.

MUSTARD MISO
vegetables

SERVES 4

8 asparagus spears

300g lotus root

300g daikon radish

1 tbsp rice wine vinegar

8 baby carrots, peeled

2 tbsp miso paste

2 tbsp grainy mustard

2 tsp caster sugar

2 tbsp soy sauce

2 tbsp mirin (sweet rice wine)

1 tbsp sesame oil

handful of baby spinach

100g enoki mushrooms, trimmed

1 tsp sesame seeds

Rich, fragrant, protein-packed miso is simply fermented soybean paste, but it is amazingly addictive. My favourite is white miso (*shiromiso*), which isn't white at all but a light caramel colour.

SNAP off the woody ends of the asparagus.

PEEL the lotus root and radish, and cut into 2cm rounds; halve the radish slices.

ADD the vinegar to a pot of simmering salted water and cook the lotus root, radish and carrots for 5 minutes.

ADD the asparagus and cook for a further 5 minutes.

WHISK the miso paste, mustard, sugar, soy, mirin and sesame oil in a bowl.

WHISK in 2 tbsp of the cooking water.

ARRANGE the baby spinach on four plates.

DRAIN the vegetables and pile on top of the spinach.

TUCK in the enoki mushrooms.

DRIZZLE the miso mustard sauce over the top.

SCATTER with sesame seeds and serve.

NUTTY QUINOA
with greens

SERVES 4

400g quinoa
10 cherry tomatoes, halved
100g baby spinach
2 tbsp pistachios or hazelnuts
2 tbsp sultanas or currants
3 tbsp mint leaves, torn
3 tbsp parsley leaves
2 tbsp extra virgin olive oil
1 tbsp lemon juice
1 tsp ground cumin
1 tsp fennel seeds
sea salt and pepper

Pronounced 'keen-wa', this ancient Inca grain is a bit like couscous, only better for you. You can tell when it's cooked because a little white tail appears on each grain.

WASH the quinoa, drain and tip into a saucepan.
COVER with 1 litre cold water and bring to the boil.
SIMMER for 10 minutes or until tender but still al dente.
DRAIN well and cool.
FLUFF up the quinoa with a fork.
TOSS with the cherry tomatoes, spinach, pistachios, sultanas, mint and parsley.
WHISK the olive oil, lemon juice, cumin and fennel seeds together and season with sea salt and pepper.
TOSS the quinoa with the dressing and serve.

AUBERGINE CURRY
with ginger and chilli

SERVES 4

800g aubergines (eggplant)

2 tbsp vegetable oil

1 onion, halved and sliced

1 green chilli, sliced

2cm knob of fresh ginger, shredded

2 garlic cloves, crushed

400g canned chopped tomatoes

1 tbsp tomato purée (paste)

good pinch of cayenne pepper

1 tsp ground coriander

1 tsp ground cumin

1 tsp sea salt

2 tbsp coriander leaves, chopped

150g natural low-fat yoghurt

Why do we need 'meat substitutes' when vegetables like aubergine are so meaty and satisfying? This north Indian *baigan bharta* is lovely with rice or lentils.

HEAT the oven to 220°C/Gas 7.

PRICK the aubergines with a fork.

BAKE in the oven for 20 minutes to char the skin.

PEEL away the skin and roughly mash or chop the flesh.

HEAT the oil in a non-stick pan.

COOK the onion until soft.

STIR in the chilli, ginger and garlic, and fry for 1 minute.

ADD the aubergine, tomatoes, tomato purée, cayenne, coriander, cumin and sea salt, stirring well.

COOK for a further 10 minutes.

SCATTER with coriander and serve with yoghurt.

SOFT POLENTA
with mushrooms

SERVES 4

1 tbsp dried wild mushrooms
750g assorted fresh mushrooms
2 tbsp olive oil
2 garlic cloves, finely sliced
2 tbsp finely chopped flat leaf
  parsley
sea salt and pepper
handful of rocket leaves

POLENTA:

500ml milk
150g instant polenta
1 tsp sea salt
1 tbsp butter
2 tbsp freshly grated parmesan

I love polenta and my husband loves mushrooms, so this recipe has a clear division of labour in our house. Use a mix of wild and cultivated fresh mushrooms for the stew – anything you can lay your hands on.

SOAK the dried mushrooms in 250ml warm water for 30 minutes.

DRAIN the mushrooms, saving the water, and slice finely.

WIPE the fresh mushrooms and slice finely.

HEAT the olive oil in a fry pan.

ADD the garlic and mushrooms (fresh and dried) and toss well.

ADD the mushroom water, parsley, sea salt and pepper.

SIMMER for 10 minutes until tender.

BRING the milk and 750ml water to the boil in a pan.

POUR in the polenta slowly, whisking constantly.

SWAP the whisk for a wooden spoon as it thickens.

STIR over gentle heat for about 6 minutes.

ADD the sea salt, butter and parmesan, stirring.

SPOON the polenta onto warm plates and top with the mushrooms and rocket.

Fast food is good food cooked in less than 30 minutes, because sometimes that's all the time we have. It isn't just the cooking that takes its toll, it's the planning, the shopping and the prepping at the end of a hard day's work.

It helps to be prepared, with a kitchen full of fast-acting foods you can call on every time you walk in the door with a fresh chicken breast or fillet of fish.

Here's my survival guide: lemons, garlic, tomatoes, free-range eggs, live yoghurt, tahini, capers, olives, almonds, balsamic vinegar, really good extra virgin olive oil, nuts, seeds, dried fruits, pumpernickel bread, Swedish crispbreads, canned tomatoes, lentils, beans, chickpeas, brown rice, couscous, curry paste, canned sweetcorn kernels, canned tuna in oil, Dijon mustard, apple cider vinegar, soy sauce, chilli sauce, paprika, horseradish sauce, maple syrup, hot lime pickle, seaweeds, fresh parmesan and dark chocolate.

Then there's the matter of delegation. If you have kids, turn them into underage kitchen apprentices and start them on cooking the stuff they like to eat – pasta, tomatoes, eggs, cheese – or washing salad greens or setting the table. It isn't just about getting dinner on the table faster, it's sharing that warm, fuzzy feeling when everyone loves the food.

But the best reason to cook fast is that food tastes better – it's as if you capture the freshness somehow, rather than cook it out. We've all seen a pan of vegetables looking bright and beautiful and bouncy, then dull and nondescript 10 minutes later – I can only imagine the same thing is happening to their nutrients as well. Which makes fast food ideal for people who like to cook, but would much rather be eating and drinking.

For years, I had a daily recipe column from Monday to Friday – the idea being you could read it, shop for it and cook it that night. My recipes had to be lighter, healthier and faster, with less ingredients to prepare.

These became my own favourite meals for all those times I'd get home starving – like quick Spanish *revueltos* of eggs scrambled with prawns and spinach, or fast roast fish with cherry tomatoes, or grilled chicken with a spiky herb sauce.

Some cooking methods are touted as being fast, but I have to wonder about them. I find stir-fries too slow to prep, tricky to cook for more than two, and quite heavy with oil, so they're not my favourites. And a microwave would slow me down too much. Compromise can be healthy, too. If it means buying a roast chicken on the way home from work to turn into an instant warm salad, for example. Whatever works, to get good food on the table.

SPANISH EGGS
with prawns

SERVES 4

200g spinach or rocket leaves
6 medium free-range eggs
sea salt and pepper
½ tsp Spanish paprika
1 tbsp olive oil
200g cooked, peeled prawns
2 garlic cloves, very finely
   sliced
1 tbsp roughly chopped
   coriander

I can't tell you the number of times this fabulous, fast *huevos revueltos* has come to my rescue after staying out too late and getting home so hungry I could eat the fridge door.

WASH the spinach leaves and shake dry.
HEAT a dry, non-stick fry pan over high heat.
ADD the spinach and toss until just wilted.
DRAIN well and lightly squeeze dry.
WHISK the eggs, sea salt, pepper and paprika in a bowl.
HEAT the olive oil in the pan.
ADD the prawns, tossing well.
THROW in the garlic and sizzle until lightly golden.
ADD the spinach and toss well over medium heat.
POUR the eggs into the pan, stirring gently.
REST the eggs for 10 seconds, then slowly push them around the pan with a wooden paddle or spoon.
TAKE off the heat while the eggs are still runny.
SCATTER with coriander and serve.

SMOKED TROUT
choucroute

SERVES 4

8 small potatoes
sea salt and pepper
1 tbsp olive oil
1 onion, finely sliced
150ml white wine (eg Riesling)
400g sauerkraut
1 tsp cumin seeds
1 tsp caraway or fennel seeds
1 tsp juniper berries
4 smoked trout fillets
2 tbsp flat parsley leaves
Dijon mustard to serve

Keep a jar of sauerkraut (irresistibly tangy fermented cabbage) on hand. Then all you have to do is add some tender smoked trout, and dinner is done.

COOK the potatoes in simmering salted water for about 15 minutes until tender; drain.

HEAT the olive oil in a pan.

ADD the onion and cook until soft.

POUR in the wine and let bubble for 2 minutes.

ADD the sauerkraut, cumin, caraway and juniper berries.

COVER and simmer for 15 minutes, adding a little water if necessary.

SLICE the potatoes thickly and add to the cabbage.

SEASON with pepper to taste.

LAY the trout on the sauerkraut, cover, and heat through for 3 minutes.

SCATTER with parsley and serve with Dijon mustard.

THAI BEEF
with lemongrass

SERVES 4

2 ribeye steaks, about 400g

1 tsp sesame oil

2 lemongrass stalks

3 red shallots, finely sliced

1 small red chilli, finely sliced

12 cherry tomatoes, halved

3 tbsp basil leaves

3 tbsp mint leaves, roughly
   chopped

3 tbsp coriander leaves

2 tbsp lime juice

2 tbsp Thai fish sauce or soy
   sauce

1 tsp sugar

1 lime, quartered

If you love a great steak, lighten up by turning it into a sizzling Thai beef salad – you'll love that too.

HEAT a ridged cast-iron grill or non-stick fry pan.

BRUSH the steaks with sesame oil.

SEAR on one side until crusty, then turn and cook briefly on the other side.

REST on a warm plate for 10 minutes.

TRIM the lemongrass to its inner, tender white part and finely slice.

PUT the lemongrass, shallots and chilli in a bowl.

ADD the tomatoes, basil, mint and coriander, and toss.

ADD the lime juice, fish sauce and sugar.

TOSS well, then tip the salad onto a large platter.

SLICE the beef and strew through the salad.

SERVE with rice and lime wedges.

SOUFFLÉ OMELETTE
with cheese and chives

SERVES 2

4 large free-range eggs,
  separated
2 tbsp milk
sea salt and pepper
2 tbsp finely snipped chives
2 tbsp freshly grated gruyère
  or parmesan
1 tsp butter

This is quite scary, the way the eggs puff up like a golden, fluffy cloud under the grill. You won't quite believe me until you do it yourself.

HEAT the grill.

WHISK the egg yolks with the milk, sea salt and pepper.

ADD most of the chives and most of the cheese.

BEAT the egg whites in another bowl, using an electric beater, until soft peaks form.

MELT the butter in a medium non-stick fry pan (suitable to put under the grill), tilting it to coat the sides.

FOLD the whisked egg whites into the yolk mix.

POUR into the pan.

COOK over a gentle heat for 2 minutes until you can run a spatula around the edges.

SCATTER the remaining cheese on top and place under the grill for 2 to 3 minutes or until set.

SLIDE onto a warm plate and cut in two.

STREW with the remaining chives and serve.

FAST ROAST FISH
with anchovies

SERVES 4

2 red onions, halved and finely
   sliced
20 cherry tomatoes
2 tbsp mixed olives (not pitted)
1 lemon, quartered
2 tbsp extra virgin olive oil
1 tbsp balsamic vinegar, plus
   extra to serve
4 thick white fish fillets (eg cod,
   gurnard, hake, snapper),
   180g each
4 anchovy fillets (in oil)
1 tbsp chopped parsley
freshly ground pepper

This is one of those throw-everything-in-the-oven meals that will help to get you through the working week without even having to think.

HEAT the oven to 220°C/Gas 7.

TOSS the onions, cherry tomatoes, olives and lemon wedges with the olive oil and balsamic vinegar.

SCATTER on a foil-lined baking tray.

BAKE for 15 minutes.

BRUSH the fish with a little oil from the anchovy jar.

PRESS an anchovy fillet on top of each fillet.

PLACE on the onions and tomatoes.

BAKE for 10 minutes or until the fish is cooked.

SCATTER with parsley and pepper.

DRIZZLE with a little extra balsamic vinegar and serve.

ZUCCHINI
crostini

SERVES 4

2 medium courgettes
(zucchini), trimmed

1 tbsp extra virgin olive oil, plus
extra for brushing

1 tbsp grated lemon zest

1 tbsp freshly grated parmesan

sea salt and pepper

2 tsp white wine vinegar

4 free-range eggs

4 thick slices sourdough bread

8 thin slices prosciutto or
jamón

Courgettes have a lovely buttery sweetness that goes well with ham and softly poached eggs. Pile it all on grilled sourdough for a meal that is instant gratification.

SHAVE the courgettes lengthways with a veggie peeler.

POUR a kettle of boiling water over them, then drain.

TOSS the courgettes with the olive oil, lemon zest, parmesan, sea salt and pepper.

HEAT the grill.

BRING 5cm of water to the boil in a wide, shallow pan.

ADD the vinegar and reduce to a simmer.

CRACK open each egg and slide it into the water.

REMOVE with a slotted spoon after 3 minutes, when the whites have set, and drain on kitchen paper.

GRILL the sourdough bread on both sides.

BRUSH with a little olive oil.

TOP with folds of prosciutto.

PILE the courgettes on top.

LAY a poached egg on each crostini.

SCATTER with sea salt and pepper and serve.

TUNA SOUVLAKI
with tahini and parsley

SERVES 4

2 ripe tomatoes, chopped

4 tbsp flat parsley leaves

2 spring (green) onions, finely
sliced

4 thick tuna steaks

1 tbsp olive oil

sea salt and pepper

1 tsp dried mint

4 pita breads

TAHINI SAUCE:

2 tbsp tahini (sesame seed paste)

2 tbsp lemon juice

½ tsp ground cumin

3 tbsp natural low-fat yoghurt

Greek souvlaki is such a good idea, it makes sense to try it with healthy fish like tuna, as well as lamb or chicken. The gloopy, calcium-rich tahini in the yoghurt sauce gives it all a real lift.

SOAK 4 wooden skewers in water to prevent burning.

WHISK the ingredients for the tahini sauce with 2 tbsp water until smooth.

THIN with a little extra water until runny, but still creamy.

TOSS the tomatoes with the parsley and spring onions.

CUT the tuna into bite-sized chunks.

THREAD onto the wooden skewers.

BRUSH with olive oil.

SEASON well and dust with dried mint.

HEAT the grill and quickly grill the pita bread.

GRILL the tuna souvlaki for 2 minutes on either side.

PLOP a spoonful of tahini onto each pita bread.

TOP with the tuna souvlaki and tomato salad to serve.

LAMB TAGLIATA
with oven-roast tomatoes

SERVES 4

½ tsp sea salt

½ tsp black pepper

1 tbsp rosemary needles,
   chopped

3 x 200g lamb rumps

olive oil for brushing

20 cherry tomatoes on the vine

100g rocket leaves

extra virgin olive oil to drizzle

In Italy, *tagliata* means 'cut'. Italians cleverly serve their steaks sliced and shared, turning a heavy meat dish into something lighter, brighter and more like a salad.

HEAT the oven to 200°C/Gas 6.

MIX the sea salt, pepper and rosemary together.

BRUSH the lamb with olive oil.

PRESS into the herb seasoning.

SEAR in a hot pan until well browned.

PLACE on a baking tray and add the tomatoes.

BAKE for 10 minutes for medium rare lamb.

REMOVE the meat and rest for 5 minutes.

SLICE the lamb and strew over a large warm platter.

SQUISH the juice of 2 roast tomatoes over the top.

SCATTER with the roast tomatoes and rocket leaves.

DRIZZLE with extra virgin olive oil and serve.

FISH IN A BAG
with fennel and orange

SERVES 4

2 medium fennel bulbs, trimmed

4 white fish fillets (eg bream, whiting, snapper, sea bass)

sea salt and pepper

1 orange, peeled and sliced, plus 2 tbsp juice

8 bay leaves

2 tbsp small black olives

4 tbsp extra virgin olive oil

2 tbsp flat parsley leaves

This must be the simplest, lightest, easiest way to cook fish – letting it steam away in a bag, like its own little spa treatment room.

HEAT the oven to 220°C/Gas 7.

CUT out four 36cm squares of foil or baking paper.

SHAVE the fennel lengthways, as finely as you can.

SCATTER the fennel shavings on the foil squares.

PLACE the fish on top and season well.

LAY the orange slices and bay leaves on the fillets.

SCATTER the olives on top.

DRIZZLE with the olive oil and 2 tbsp orange juice.

BRING the two opposite sides of the foil up and tightly seal in a half-moon shape.

BAKE for 10 minutes for thin fillets, up to 15 minutes for thick ones.

OPEN the bags and lift the contents onto warm plates.

DRIZZLE with the juices and scatter with parsley.

GRILLED CHICKEN
with salsa verde

SERVES 4

4 chicken breasts, skin on
1 tbsp olive oil
sea salt and pepper
400g fine green beans

SALSA VERDE:

1 cup (30g) flat leaf parsley
1 cup (30g) basil or coriander
  leaves
1 garlic clove, crushed
1 tbsp tiny salted capers, rinsed
1 tbsp red wine vinegar
freshly ground black pepper
5 tbsp extra virgin olive oil

Italy's famous green sauce is so punchy, peppery and tangy that it makes anything taste interesting – even an uninspiring chicken breast.

WHIZ the herbs for the salsa verde in a blender.
ADD the garlic, capers, vinegar and pepper, and whiz.
DRIZZLE in the olive oil slowly, with the motor running.
THIN with a little water until it pours easily.
HEAT the grill.
BRUSH the chicken with olive oil.
GRILL gently until cooked through, about 15 minutes, turning once.
SEASON well and leave to rest in a warm place.
COOK the green beans in simmering salted water for 4 minutes.
DRAIN and pile onto warm plates.
SLICE the chicken and arrange on the beans.
SPOON the dressing over the chicken and serve.

Made from cooked, pressed soybeans, tofu is high in protein and minerals, low in kilojoules and easy to digest. It just needs a boot kick of flavour. For **SWEET CHILLI TOFU:** mix 1 tbsp fish sauce, 1 tbsp soy sauce, 1 tbsp sweet chilli sauce, 1 tbsp tomato purée (paste), 1 diced tomato, 1 crushed garlic clove, 2 star anise, 1 tsp sugar and 3 tbsp water. Bring to the boil, stir and simmer for 2 minutes. Cut 500g Chinese tofu into 8 squares and pat dry. Fry with 2 tsp oil for 2 minutes each side until golden. Drain well, stack two on each plate and top with the sauce. For 4.

Firmer than Japanese silken tofu, fresh Chinese tofu is better for stir-fries, curries and pan-frying. For **SPICY TOFU:** heat 1 tbsp oyster sauce, 2 tbsp soy sauce, 2 tbsp Chinese rice wine, 2 tsp sesame oil and 125ml chicken or vegetable stock in a fry pan. Add 2 sliced garlic cloves, 1 sliced red chilli, 1 sliced spring (green) onion and 1 tbsp grated ginger. Simmer, stirring, for 2 minutes. Add 500g block of fresh Chinese tofu and simmer for 3 minutes on each side. Transfer the tofu to a plate, pour the hot sauce over and cut into cubes. For 4.

TOFU X4

Silken tofu is white, soft and delicate, like a set custard – ideal for soups and steaming. It's also incredibly refreshing served icy cold on a really hot day. (Keep all fresh tofu chilled and eat as soon as possible or within 2 days, changing the water each day.) For **ICED SILKEN TOFU:** drain 300g well-chilled silken tofu and cut into four rounds with a cookie cutter. Top each tofu round with 1 tsp tobiko (flying fish roe) or salmon caviar and a pinch of finely sliced toasted nori. Serve with a little bowl of soy sauce for dipping. For 4 as a starter.

For a light and lovely weekday lunch, make a **SIMPLE TOFU SOUP** to have with take-away sushi. Combine 800ml water, 10g instant dashi, 1 tbsp mirin and 1 tbsp soy sauce in a pan and bring to a simmer. Put 2 tbsp red miso in a small bowl and whisk in a little of the hot broth, then whisk back into the dashi broth. Add 200g ready-to-eat udon noodles and 200g cubed silken tofu. Gently heat through, then throw in 100g baby spinach leaves and ladle into small bowls or mugs. Scatter with sesame seeds and serve. For 4.

Slow food is comfort food, because slow food is relaxed food. Sitting down to a roast, a simmering chicken stew, or a spicy lentil pie with a sweet potato crust is time out for the body and the mind.

When I have been running around all day and I'm all stressed out, I need food that will calm me down, not pep me up. Slow-cooked food has a depth of flavour and a melting tenderness that you just can't get in a hurry.

I remember what it was like to get home from school and smell the ham and pea soup simmering on the stove, or the roast sizzling away in the oven: I only wish I had appreciated Mum's efforts a bit more, now I know what its like to work every day and cook every night.

Slow cooking has a different set of rules that have to be learnt – like the art of simmering. In a light broth, a simmer is a visible shimmer on the surface. In a rich soup, it's a bubble rising to the surface every couple of seconds. In a thick stew, it's an occasional plop on the surface. Literally, it is liquid kept at a heat just below boiling point in a state of subdued activity, hot enough to cause the coagulation of protein, but not hot enough to break the surface with any great movement.

Braising is the low cooking of meat and vegetables with very little liquid, achieved by cooking in a lidded pan so that an intense, steamy heat is created.

In slow cooking, flavours are layered, rather than jumbled. The base flavour is usually onions, leeks, garlic and other aromatics. Meat is browned, which adds a caramelised flavour to the pan, then wine, broth or water is introduced and gently simmered – never boiled. If you end up with tough meat and dull greens, the heat was too high. Next, you throw in your beans, lentils, etc, for bulk, tomatoes for acidity, and vegetables for sweetness.

Tough herbs like rosemary and thyme can go in early, but gentle, soft-leaved herbs are added at the end for freshness. Save leafy green veg until the end, too. Shred them and stir through in the last 5 minutes. Suddenly that brown stew has colour and crunch and looks incredibly fresh.

When you're cooking large pieces of meat or whole fish, start them in cold liquid and bring gently to a simmer, so the inside has a chance to cook in the same time as the outside. Small pieces cook more evenly if you add them to an already simmering brew.

The beauty of slow food is that you can leave it alone to cook by itself, while you do something else, like go for a slow walk or read a book. Don't pester the food, just let it cook. That way, you have a chance of being almost as relaxed as your dinner.

GREEK MEATBALLS
with tomato sauce

SERVES 4

2 thick slices white bread, crust
   removed
125ml red wine
500g minced beef or lamb
1 small onion, grated
2 garlic cloves, crushed
½ beaten egg
1 tbsp chopped parsley
1 tsp ground cumin
½ tsp ground cinnamon
sea salt and pepper
500ml tomato passata
2 tbsp tomato purée (paste)
2 tbsp tomato ketchup
1 tbsp olive oil
1 tsp sugar
2 bay leaves
handful of rocket leaves

Fried meatballs can be small, heavy and oily – so bake rather than fry, for big, light, bouncy meatballs instead. Serve with rice and a big Greek salad.

HEAT the oven to 180°C/Gas 4.

TEAR the bread into pieces.

SOAK in the wine for 5 minutes, then squeeze lightly, reserving the wine.

MIX the bread with the minced meat, onion, 1 crushed garlic clove, egg, parsley, spices, sea salt and pepper.

MULCH with your hands to mix well.

SHAPE into nice big balls and bake for 20 minutes.

PUT the wine, passata, tomato purée, ketchup, olive oil, remaining garlic, sugar and bay leaves in a saucepan.

STIR well and simmer for 20 minutes until thick.

ADD the meatballs to the tomato sauce and simmer for 10 minutes.

STREW with rocket and serve.

ZEN CHICKEN
with daikon

SERVES 4

300g daikon (long white radish)
8 fresh shiitake mushrooms
1 litre instant dashi (page 213)
60ml soy sauce or tamari
60ml mirin (sweet rice wine)
2 medium carrots, sliced
500g chicken breasts, skinned
150g lotus root
100g dried udon noodles
sea salt
100g baby spinach

Cooking this light, subtle *nimono* (simmered) dish after a busy day makes me slow down and feel as close to serene as I will ever get.

PEEL the daikon, halve lengthways and slice thickly.
CUT off the stalks and halve the mushrooms.
COMBINE the dashi, soy and mirin in a pan and heat.
ADD the daikon, carrots, chicken and mushrooms.
PEEL and finely slice the lotus root.
ADD to the pan and simmer very gently for 30 minutes until everything is tender, skimming occasionally.
COOK the noodles in a pan of simmering salted water for 8 minutes until al dente, then drain.
REMOVE the chicken from the broth and thickly slice.
ARRANGE the noodles, vegetables and chicken in four warm shallow bowls.
SCATTER with baby spinach leaves.
STRAIN the hot broth over the top and serve.

BRAISED SQUID
with tomato and peas

SERVES 4

1kg medium squid, cleaned
3 tbsp olive oil
1 onion, halved and finely sliced
2 garlic cloves, crushed
125ml dry white wine
400g can tomatoes or 400ml
   passata
125ml water or stock
½ tsp paprika
sea salt and pepper
200g green peas, fresh or frozen
2 tbsp flat parsley leaves

Squid – or calamari – is one of those things you cook either very quickly or very slowly, because anything between is a rubbery disaster. This is the slow way.

CUT the squid bodies into thick rings.
HEAT the olive oil in a heavy-based pan.
ADD the onion and cook gently for 10 minutes.
TOSS in the garlic and stir for 30 seconds.
ADD the squid and fry gently for 3 minutes until it is lightly coloured.
POUR in the wine and let bubble for a minute or two.
ADD the tomatoes, water, paprika, sea salt and pepper.
SIMMER over the lowest possible heat for 40 minutes.
COOK the peas in boiling salted water for 5 minutes.
DRAIN and add to the squid.
SIMMER for 10 minutes.
SCATTER with parsley and serve.

BRAISED OXTAIL
with ginger and chilli

SERVES 4

1kg oxtail, in chunks

2 tbsp plain flour

3 tbsp vegetable oil

1 onion, thickly sliced

knob of fresh ginger, finely
  sliced

4 garlic cloves, finely sliced

1 to 2 green chillies, sliced

50ml Chinese rice wine or
  dry sherry

50ml soy sauce

2 star anise

1 cinnamon stick

sea salt and pepper

1 tbsp soft brown sugar

3 tbsp coriander leaves,
  chopped

My mum is an expert on long, slow, do-ahead cooking, because she would rather be at the table having fun, than in the kitchen, working. It must be hereditary.

HEAT the oven to 160°C/Gas 3.

DUST the oxtail pieces with flour.

HEAT half the oil in a heavy ovenproof pan.

COOK the onion, ginger, garlic and chilli for 10 minutes.

REMOVE and add the remaining oil to the pan.

BROWN the oxtail pieces well on both sides.

ADD the rice wine and bring to the boil.

RETURN the onion mix to the pan and add the soy, star anise, cinnamon, sea salt, pepper and sugar.

ADD enough hot water to just cover the oxtail.

BRING to a simmer, stirring.

COVER and cook in the oven for 2½ to 3 hours, giving the meat an occasional poke and a stir.

COOL and skim off any fat.

REHEAT gently, stir in the chopped coriander and serve.

LAMB TAGINE
with dates

SERVES 4

1kg boned shoulder of lamb
300g large carrots
1 tbsp olive oil
1 onion, halved and finely sliced
½ tsp cayenne pepper
½ tsp ground saffron
1 tsp ground ginger
1 tsp ground turmeric
2 cinnamon sticks
1 tbsp tomato purée (paste)
100g dried apricots
1 tbsp honey
1 tsp orange flower water
sea salt and pepper
8 soft, pitted Medjool dates
2 tbsp flat parsley leaves

This is Terry's own personal tagine, which he always serves with couscous, spicy harissa and a glass of Pinot Noir. Consider yourself honoured.

CUT the lamb into 4cm cubes.

CUT the carrots into 5cm lengths; quarter lengthways.

HEAT the olive oil in a large heavy-based pan.

COOK the onion for 5 minutes.

ADD the lamb, carrots and spices.

POUR in enough water to just cover the lamb.

BRING to just under the boil, skimming if necessary.

STIR in the tomato purée.

SIMMER very gently for 1 hour and 20 minutes.

ADD the apricots to the pan with the honey, orange flower water, sea salt and pepper.

SIMMER for 20 minutes until thick and soupy.

ADD the dates and simmer for 5 minutes.

SCATTER with parsley leaves and serve.

KOREAN
bibimbap

SERVES 4

300g rib-eye steak fillet

2 tbsp soy sauce

1 tbsp sesame oil

sea salt and pepper

400g jasmine rice, rinsed

50g baby spinach, well washed

2 tsp olive oil

½ cucumber, cut into fine
matchsticks

½ carrot, cut into fine
matchsticks

1 tbsp sesame seeds

SAUCE:

2 tbsp thick chilli sauce or
Korean gochujang

2 garlic cloves, crushed

2 tbsp soy sauce

2 tsp rice vinegar

2 tsp sugar

2 tsp sesame oil

Bibim means 'to stir through' and *bap* means rice, so don't forget to *bibim* your *bap* at the table.

MARINATE the rib-eye steak with the soy, sesame oil, sea salt and pepper.

PUT the rice and 700ml water in a lidded cooking pot.

BRING to the boil and cover tightly.

REDUCE the heat to very low and cook for 20 minutes.

BEAT the sauce ingredients in a small bowl.

PUT the spinach in a dry, non-stick pan and toss over high heat until just wilted.

HEAT a little olive oil in a fry pan or griddle.

SEAR the steak until crusty outside, rare inside.

FILL four hot deep bowls with the hot rice.

PILE the spinach on top.

SLICE the steak and arrange over the spinach with the cucumber and carrot.

SPOON over the sauce and scatter with sesame seeds.

WINTER GREENS
with chicken and beans

SERVES 4

250g winter greens, well washed

1 tbsp olive oil

4 chicken drumsticks

2 chicken breasts, with skin

sea salt and pepper

1 onion, finely sliced

2 garlic cloves, crushed

600g canned borlotti beans, rinsed

few thyme sprigs, plus extra to serve

500ml hot vegetable or chicken stock

Green leafy vegetables are famously good for us – and the darker the green, the better. Look for cavolo nero, Swiss chard, kale, spring greens, sprouting broccoli or Savoy cabbage.

SHRED the greens roughly.

HEAT the olive oil in a large lidded fry pan.

SEAR the chicken, skin-side down, for 5 minutes on each side, until golden.

REMOVE the chicken, season well and set aside.

COOK the onion in the pan for 5 minutes until softened.

ADD the garlic and cook for 1 minute.

STIR in the beans, thyme, stock, sea salt and pepper.

RETURN the chicken to the pan and cover with the lid.

SIMMER gently for 30 minutes or until cooked.

ADD the shredded greens and simmer for 5 minutes.

CUT the chicken breasts in half.

MASH a few beans into the sauce to thicken it.

SCATTER with fresh thyme and serve on warm plates.

SWEET POTATO
and lentil pie

SERVES 4

1 tbsp olive oil
1 onion, finely chopped
3 celery stalks, finely chopped
3 carrots, chopped
2 garlic cloves, finely sliced
400g can chopped tomatoes
1 tbsp tomato purée (paste)
2 bay leaves
1 tsp paprika
200g Puy lentils, rinsed
750g orange-fleshed sweet
  potatoes
sea salt and pepper
2 tbsp finely chopped parsley
freshly grated nutmeg
1 tbsp freshly grated parmesan

When you grow up on a sheep farm, you carry the craving for shepherd's pie in your genes. Now I like this veggo version just as much – but I still have to have it with tomato sauce.

HEAT the olive oil in a fry pan and cook the onion, celery, carrots and garlic for 5 to 10 minutes to soften.
ADD the tomatoes, tomato purée, bay leaves, paprika, lentils and 1.5 litres water, stirring.
SIMMER for 30 minutes or until tender, thick and soupy.
HEAT the oven to 200°C/Gas 6.
PEEL the sweet potatoes and cut into large chunks.
SIMMER in salted water for about 15 minutes until soft.
ADD the parsley, sea salt and pepper to the lentils.
SPOON into a pie dish.
DRAIN the sweet potatoes well.
MASH with nutmeg, parmesan, sea salt and pepper.
SPREAD the mash over the top of the lentils.
BAKE for 20 minutes until bubbling, and serve.

BARLEY RISOTTO
with cauliflower

SERVES 4

1 cauliflower, trimmed
750ml hot vegetable or chicken
    stock
2 tbsp olive oil
1 onion, finely chopped
1 carrot, finely diced
200g pearl barley
125ml dry white wine
sea salt and pepper
1 tbsp butter
2 tbsp freshly grated parmesan
2 tbsp flat parsley or sage leaves
2 tbsp toasted walnuts

Nutty-tasting pearl (hulled) barley makes a brilliant risotto because it needs no soaking, just an occasional stir as it cooks, to help it on its way.

CUT the cauliflower into small florets and dice the stalks.
HEAT the olive oil in a heavy-based pan.
ADD the onion, carrot and diced cauliflower stalk.
COOK, stirring, until the onion is soft.
ADD the pearl barley and toss well to coat.
POUR in the wine, stir and let bubble until well reduced.
STIR in the cauliflower florets and most of the hot stock.
COVER and simmer gently, stirring occasionally, for 30 to 35 minutes until the stock is absorbed and all is tender.
ADD the remaining stock, sea salt and pepper, stirring.
STIR in the butter and parmesan.
SCATTER with parsley and walnuts to serve.

Umami is a vaguely savoury, brothy taste isolated by the Japanese as the 'fifth taste', after salty, sour, sweet and bitter. Found in foods with natural glutamates, like mushrooms, miso, parmesan and nori seaweed, it has instant sex appeal. For **PORCINI-DUSTED EGGS:** whiz 20g dried porcini, ceps or shiitake mushrooms and a pinch of sea salt to a powder in a coffee grinder. Heat 1 tsp olive oil in a fry pan, break in 2 eggs and cook, covered, over a low heat for 4 minutes. Transfer to warm plates, dust each egg with a scant teaspoon of porcini dust and serve on grilled sourdough bread. For 2.

Parmesan is the most beautiful cheese in the world, with a fulfilling, umami-rich flavour that makes it my number one desert island food. Make snappy little **PARMESAN CRISPS** to serve with soups and salads. Mix 30g grated parmesan with 2 tsp plain flour and a little pepper. Form into 8 discs on a baking sheet lined with baking paper (using a biscuit cutter to shape them). Bake at 180°C/Gas 4 for 7 to 8 minutes. Cool slightly, then peel off the paper and cool on a wire rack. Toss 100g mustard cress or baby green leaves in 1 tsp olive oil and sandwich between 2 parmesan crisps. For 4.

UMAMI X4

Miso, or Japanese soybean paste, is naturally rich in umami. White miso is lightly fermented and tastes sweet and light, while red miso is stronger and saltier. Go beyond miso soup and use it as a marinade, a dip and a salad dressing. A tablespoon of miso will also add instant umami to a beef stew or warming vegetable and barley soup. For **MISO LAMB CHOPS:** mix 2 tbsp white or red miso paste with 2 tbsp soy and 1 tbsp mirin. Spread on 10 well-trimmed lamb cutlets, marinate for a while, then grill or barbecue. This is also good with barbecued chicken and fish. For 4.

What else has umami? Tomatoes, anchovies, soy sauce, truffles, green tea and tuna. For a double whammy, try **SPICY TUNA NORI ROLLS:** finely dice 200g sashimi-quality tuna fillet and toss with ½ tsp Japanese togarashi pepper. Peel an avocado, cut into finger-length strips and toss in 1 tbsp lemon juice. Lightly toast 4 nori sheets to crisp them, then cut in half. Arrange 1 tbsp spicy tuna, a small handful of baby alfalfa sprouts and 2 avocado fingers on each nori sheet, season and roll into fat cylinders, sealing the edge with sesame oil. Makes 8 rolls.

Easy food is the stuff you need to get you through the working week. Recipes that fit into your life, not recipes you have to fit your life around.

In our house, Monday night suppers are usually a simple soup or a snacky egg dish. By Tuesday I'm looking forward to fresh fish because the seafood markets are up and running again. On Wednesday, I need a spicy Indian, or a quick pasta – comfort food I can do without having to think. Thursday might be a simple supper with a couple of mates, and Friday – if we stay in – is a great time to relax over a few drinks and try something a bit glam.

The starting point, when you need to do something easy, is something familiar. Take the dishes you grew up with and give them a twist, making them easier to do and lighter to eat. Instead of a big roast, do a little one, tossing a few halved poussins (baby chickens) in a pan with chunky potatoes and roasting them together until golden. Rather than meat burgers, do fresh salmon burgers. Instead of pasta with a meat sauce, do spaghetti with tomatoes, olives, chilli and rocket. Swap the slow-cooked Indian curry for a fast-cooked savoury mince – kheema with peas. You just want something delicious that won't take too much energy to produce, to eat, or to clean up afterwards.

Easy food is often, but not always, fast. Sometimes it is easier to get something started and go off and leave it alone to cook itself for half an hour. But most recipes in this chapter fall into the sear-it-in-a-pan or chuck-it-in-the-oven schools of cooking. Take a fresh fish fillet, wrap it with a slice of prosciutto, sear it in a pan and serve it on a bed of broad beans or asparagus. Do the same with chicken breast. Or sizzle sliced haloumi cheese to serve with seafood or salad. Or turn on the oven, pour yourself a glass of wine, and whiz up some little quiches (do extra for an office lunch or a picnic) or spicy chicken wings. Just good, everyday food you can make over and over again, until it is a part of family history.

It's all so effortless now that our shops are full of such good things to grab on the way home. Treat yourself to the best ingredients, full of flavour and freshness, and cooking is easy. It's trying to turn highly processed foods and exotic out-of-season produce into a great meal that's hard.

Form your own definition of what is easy and what is good – don't let your shopping be influenced by heavily advertised 'convenience' foods. There are enough genuinely convenient foods around, like eggs, canned tomatoes, cheeses, cured meats, instant polenta and frozen peas, that don't compromise your good taste.

PAPER-WRAPPED
quiches

SERVES 4 / MAKES 8

400g spinach, well washed

6 large eggs

100ml milk

2 tbsp freshly grated parmesan
  or gruyère, plus 1 extra tbsp

sea salt and pepper

2 tbsp finely chopped chives or
  parsley

2 thick slices ham, diced

8 cherry tomatoes, halved

These little tarts don't need pastry at all. Instead, they cook in a scrunch of baking paper, so they're easier to make and lighter to take for office lunches, fast suppers and picnics.

COOK the spinach in a dry non-stick pan over high heat until wilted, tossing well.

SQUEEZE dry and set aside.

HEAT the oven to 180°C/Gas 4.

CUT eight 15cm baking paper squares.

LINE 8 deep muffin moulds with the squares.

BEAT the eggs with the milk, 2 tbsp cheese, sea salt, pepper and chives.

SCATTER a little spinach and ham into each mould.

FILL with the egg mixture.

TOP each one with two cherry tomato halves.

BAKE for 12 to 15 minutes until just set.

TOP with extra grated cheese.

EAT warm, or cool.

STICKY CHICKEN
wings

SERVES 4

8 organic chicken wings
1 tbsp grated fresh ginger
1 garlic clove, crushed
2 tbsp soy sauce
2 tbsp Chinese rice wine or
   dry sherry
2 tbsp oyster sauce
sea salt and pepper
2 tbsp honey
1 tsp five-spice powder
1 tsp sesame oil
2 spring (green) onions, finely
   sliced
1 lime, quartered
sweet chilli sauce for dipping

Another triumph for common sense: these spicy golden chicken wings are roasted instead of deep-fried, for a much lighter result – they taste so much better this way.

TOSS the chicken wings in a bowl with the ginger, garlic, soy, rice wine, oyster sauce, sea salt, pepper, honey, five-spice and sesame oil.

LEAVE to marinate for 30 minutes or so.

HEAT the oven to 200°C/Gas 6.

DRAIN the chicken wings.

ARRANGE on a baking tray lined with baking paper.

BAKE for 20 to 30 minutes or until golden brown.

SCATTER the chicken with spring onions.

SERVE with limes for squeezing, and sweet chilli sauce for dipping.

FRESH SALMON
burgers

SERVES 4

600g fresh organic salmon fillet

1 shallot, finely minced

1 tsp salted capers, rinsed

1 tsp grated lemon zest

1 tbsp finely chopped parsley
  or dill

dash of Tabasco

dash of Worcestershire sauce

1 tsp Dijon mustard

sea salt and pepper

1 small egg white, beaten

1 tbsp olive oil

2 dill pickles, sliced lengthways

1 bunch of watercress, washed

There is nothing wrong with the idea of a burger – it's what the world has done with it that is shameful. Made with fresh salmon and lightly cooked, it's a proper treat.

CHOP the salmon fillet finely, removing the skin and any pin bones.

MIX with the shallot, capers, lemon zest and parsley.

ADD the Tabasco, Worcestershire sauce, mustard, sea salt, pepper and egg white.

MULCH everything together with your hands.

FORM into four flat, large patties.

REFRIGERATE for 30 minutes to help them set.

HEAT the olive oil in a fry pan.

SEAR the burgers on one side until golden.

TURN gently and cook to your liking.

SERVE with the dill pickles and watercress.

SIZZLING HALOUMI
with prawns

SERVES 4

200g haloumi cheese, rinsed
2 tbsp extra virgin olive oil
200g cherry tomatoes
16 small or 12 medium raw
  prawns, peeled and deveined
1 lemon, quartered

DRESSING:

1 tbsp lemon juice
2 tbsp extra virgin olive oil
2 tbsp green olives
8 caper berries
1 tsp tiny salted capers, rinsed
1 tbsp finely chopped dill

Haloumi is a rich, salty Greek-Cypriot cheese that is inedible cold, delicious when hot, and dead boring when it has gone cold again. So serve it hot.

CUT the haloumi into four 1cm thick slices.

MIX the dressing ingredients together in a bowl.

HEAT 1 tbsp olive oil in a non-stick pan.

COOK the cherry tomatoes for 3 minutes, then remove.

ADD the remaining olive oil to the pan.

COOK the prawns over high heat until they are no longer translucent, turning once.

WIPE out the pan and return to the heat.

SIZZLE the haloumi on one side only until golden.

ARRANGE the sizzling haloumi on warm plates.

TOP with the prawns and tomatoes.

DRIZZLE with the green olive dressing.

SERVE with lemon wedges.

POLLO ARROSTO
con patate

SERVES 4

800g medium all-purpose
   potatoes
1 red onion, cut into wedges
2 tbsp olive oil, plus extra to
   drizzle
1 tsp dried oregano
1 tbsp thyme leaves
sea salt and pepper
200ml dry white wine
4 poussins (small chickens),
   about 450g each
12 cherry tomatoes on the vine
oregano and thyme leaves
   to serve

I love the way cafes at Italian airports cook great quantities of food in huge baking trays without any fuss. This is roast chicken and chips, Venice airport style.

HEAT the oven to 220°C/Gas 7.

PEEL the potatoes, halve lengthways and slice thickly.

TOSS with the onion, olive oil, herbs, sea salt and pepper.

SCATTER over the base of a large, oiled roasting pan.

POUR over the wine and 200ml water.

ROAST for 20 minutes.

CUT each poussin in half, firmly down one side of the backbone, with a strong knife.

ADD them to the roasting pan and drizzle with olive oil.

ROAST for 20 minutes, shooshing the potatoes around once or twice to prevent sticking.

ADD the tomatoes and roast for another 20 minutes.

STREW with oregano and thyme leaves and drizzle with the pan juices.

SERVE with a rocket or watercress salad.

FISH
saltimbocca

SERVES 4

4 white fish fillets (eg cod, whiting, gurnard, hake, ling), skinned
sea salt and pepper
8 wide slices prosciutto or jamón
8 sage leaves
400g podded peas or broad beans (or a mixture)
400g asparagus, trimmed
1 tbsp olive oil

We know we should eat more fish, but night after night, it can get a bit boring. Here, the prosciutto protects the fish and gives it a crisp, salty bite that turns it into something else again.

TRIM the fish into 8 oblong fingers and season with sea salt and pepper.

WRAP each finger in prosciutto, leaving the ends free.

PLACE a sage leaf on each one.

COOK the peas and/or broad beans and asparagus in simmering salted water for 4 minutes.

HEAT half the olive oil in a fry pan.

COOK the fish, sage-side down, for 3 minutes until the prosciutto is crisp.

TURN and cook for 2 minutes or more, depending on thickness.

DRAIN the vegetables and toss with the remaining olive oil, sea salt and pepper.

TOP with the fish and serve.

FISH
in crazy water

SERVES 4

1 tbsp olive oil
2 garlic cloves, finely sliced
1 mild red chilli, finely sliced
4 fish cutlets on the bone
   (eg cod, hake, snapper)
4 bay leaves
100ml dry white wine
400ml light stock or water
½ tsp sea salt
20 cherry tomatoes, halved
20 small black olives
1 tbsp small salted capers,
   rinsed
pinch of dried chilli flakes
2 tbsp basil leaves
1 tbsp extra virgin olive oil

In Southern Italy, whole fish are poached in water made 'crazy' with chilli. I do it with cutlets – the best come from the middle of the fish, just behind the gut cavity, where they are nice and round (not horseshoe-shaped).

HEAT the olive oil in a fry pan and add the sliced garlic and chilli.

ADD the fish cutlets and fry for 2 minutes or until golden.

TURN the fish over, add the bay leaves, wine, stock and sea salt, and bring to a simmer.

SIMMER gently for 10 minutes or until cooked.

TRANSFER the fish to four warm shallow bowls.

ADD the tomatoes, olives, capers and chilli flakes to the pan and simmer for 2 minutes.

SPOON the 'crazy water' over the fish and tomatoes.

SCATTER the basil leaves over.

DRIZZLE with extra virgin olive oil and serve.

KHEEMA
with peas

SERVES 4

2 tbsp vegetable oil

2 onions, finely chopped

1 tbsp grated fresh ginger

2 garlic cloves, crushed

1 tsp ground coriander

½ tsp dried chilli flakes

1 tsp turmeric

750g lean minced lamb or beef

2 tbsp tomato purée (paste)

250ml stock or water

½ tsp sea salt

¼ tsp pepper

200g podded fresh or frozen peas

1 to 2 tsp garam masala

3 tbsp coriander leaves, chopped

Kheema is a fast, easy savoury mince that's a good way to introduce the kids to a bit of spice. Serve with a drizzle of yoghurt, and rice or lentils.

HEAT the oil in a fry pan.

COOK the onions gently for 5 minutes until lightly golden.

STIR in the ginger, garlic and spices.

ADD the meat and fry for 5 minutes until browned.

STIR in the tomato purée, stock, sea salt and pepper.

COVER and cook gently for 20 minutes.

ADD the peas and simmer for 5 minutes or until cooked.

STIR in garam masala to taste.

SCATTER with chopped coriander and serve.

SPAGHETTI
alla puttanesca

SERVES 4

350g spaghetti or spaghettini
2 tbsp olive oil
2 garlic cloves, finely sliced
4 anchovy fillets in oil, drained
400g canned cherry tomatoes
2 tbsp small black olives
good pinch of dried chilli flakes
2 tbsp small salted capers, rinsed
½ tsp dried oregano
1 tbsp finely chopped parsley
sea salt and pepper
2 tbsp flat parsley leaves

This was allegedly the pasta dish hurriedly made by Neapolitan working girls between clients. Sounds like something all working girls would find useful.

COOK the spaghetti in plenty of boiling salted water until al dente.

HEAT the olive oil in a fry pan and gently cook the garlic for a minute or two.

ADD the anchovies and soften them in the oil.

STIR in the cherry tomatoes, olives, chilli flakes, capers and oregano.

COOK over medium heat for 5 minutes, stirring often.

STIR in 3 tbsp of the pasta cooking water.

ADD the chopped parsley, sea salt and pepper.

DRAIN the pasta and toss with the sauce.

SCATTER with parsley leaves and serve.

HARISSA BEEF
with couscous

SERVES 4

600g beef fillet, rolled and tied

1 tbsp harissa

1 tbsp olive oil

300g couscous

1 red onion, halved and finely
   sliced

1 tbsp extra virgin olive oil

1 tsp ground cinnamon

1 tsp ground cumin

1 tsp ground coriander

sea salt and pepper

600g asparagus or green beans,
   trimmed

2 tbsp coriander leaves

Fast and foolproof, couscous makes a great bed for crusty beef spiced up with garlicky, blow-your-socks-off North African harissa chilli paste.

HEAT the oven to 200°C/Gas 6.

COAT the beef with the harissa.

HEAT the olive oil in a non-stick fry pan.

SEAR the beef on all sides until browned.

TRANSFER to the oven and cook for 20 minutes.

REMOVE the beef, cover with foil and rest for 10 minutes.

TOSS the couscous with the red onion, extra virgin olive oil, spices, sea salt and pepper in a heatproof bowl.

POUR 500ml boiling water over the couscous, cover with foil and leave in the switched-off oven for 10 minutes.

COOK the asparagus in simmering salted water for 5 minutes, then drain.

ARRANGE the asparagus on the couscous.

SCATTER with coriander leaves.

SLICE the beef thickly and arrange on top.

The best thing about steaming is that everything tastes so squeaky clean and natural. What goes into the steamer comes out intact, without leaving all of its flavour behind in the water.

The steam condenses on the surface of the food and seals it faster than if it were boiled, retaining its juices and goodness. And there is very little need for oil or fat. But what I really love is how good the food looks in all its bright steaminess.

Steaming is brilliant for delicate seafood like prawns, scallops and oysters; for couscous, green vegetables, egg dishes, Chinese dumplings and stuffed tofu; and for individual steamed puddings. A small potato steamed in its skin tastes much better than one peeled, chopped and boiled in water.

For years, I owned a simple Chinese steamer that just sat on the stove. I noticed if I put it away on top of the cupboard, I never steamed anything, but if it was out in full view, I steamed more. Lesson learned.

Now I have a two-tier stainless steel electric steamer that will steam everything in sight. It's enormously pleasing, not to mention energy-efficient, to cook the whole meal in the steamer. For one of my favourite fast meals, I steam small whole potatoes for 15 minutes, then add salmon fillets for 5 minutes, and spinach leaves for another 2 minutes. Done.

Most people think of steaming as being gentle and soothing. I did, too, until I kept scalding myself as I lifted the lid to rearrange the food. Now I use my longest tongs to get in and out, but it made me aware of what the food was going through and how easy it was to overcook everything, including me.

Having a see-through top on a steamer is better than an automatic timer, because you can see every stage of the cooking process. Just take vegetables out when they are looking their brightest and greenest. If you marinate fish or meat, then steam it in the marinade for an instant sauce as well.

If you don't have a steamer, you can still steam. I cook my rice in an ordinary saucepan with a tight-fitting lid – but that's steaming. Wrapping food in foil and baking it in the oven is, in effect, steaming. Individual puddings covered with foil and cooked in a water-bath in the oven are steamed, as if they were in a steamer.

When steaming: keep the pan one-third full of water, checking the level every so often. Be careful that what is on one tier doesn't drip down to spoil the food below. Put the most delicate foods on the top tier, furthest from the water. If you line the rack with baking paper, pierce it a few times with a skewer to allow the steam through.

One last good use: warm your plates in the steamer just before serving.

LE GRAND
aïoli

SERVES 4

800g thick-flaked white fish
   fillet (eg Icelandic cod, blue-
   eye cod)
20g sea salt flakes
600g baby potatoes, unpeeled
bunch of baby carrots, peeled
300g fine green beans, topped
3 tbsp small black olives
2 tbsp finely snipped chives
2 to 4 hard-boiled eggs, halved
200g cherry tomatoes on the
   vine, or 4 tomatoes,
   quartered
freshly ground black pepper
100ml aïoli (page 214)

Steam up a Provençal feast of lightly salted fish and vegetables, add eggs, tomatoes and garlicky aïoli, and serve hot, warm or at room temperature, depending on the weather.

PLACE the fish in a shallow dish and scatter with sea salt.
COVER with cling film and refrigerate for 24 hours, turning once.
RINSE thoroughly in cold water and pat dry.
SET up a two-level steamer over simmering water.
STEAM the potatoes for 10 minutes.
ADD the carrots and steam for a further 5 minutes.
ADD the beans to the vegetables and place the fish in the upper steamer basket.
STEAM for 5 minutes or until the fish flakes easily.
REMOVE the skin and break the fish into large pieces.
SLICE the potatoes and toss with the olives and chives.
ARRANGE the fish, potatoes, carrots, beans, eggs and tomatoes on four dinner plates.
ADD black pepper and serve with aïoli.

SPRING ONION
scallops

SERVES 4

8 sea scallops on their shell

100g spring (green) onions,
   green part only

2 garlic cloves, finely grated

2 tsp finely grated fresh ginger

1 tbsp soy sauce

1 tbsp vegetable oil

1 tbsp sesame oil

sea salt and pepper

The joy of this pretty first course is the wild green taste of the spring onions. If they don't come with their long green stems intact, yell very loudly at your greengrocer.

SET your steamer going on high.

TRIM the scallops, wash, pat dry and return to the shell.

CHOP the spring onions finely, or whiz briefly in a food processor.

MIX with the garlic, ginger, soy, oils, sea salt and pepper.

SPOON over each scallop.

STEAM for 2 to 3 minutes, depending on size.

SERVE the scallops as a first course, or as part of an Asian meal, with rice.

CHAWAN
mushi

SERVES 4

8 small prawns
100g fresh salmon fillet
sea salt
8 small mangetout (snow peas)
4 fresh shiitake mushrooms
4 free-range eggs (60 to 65g)
600ml Japanese dashi broth
  (page 213)
2 tbsp mirin (sweet rice wine)
few coriander leaves to finish

The epitome of soft, steamy goodness, this gossamer-light savoury custard is a Japanese family favourite. It is often more complex than this, but I can't do complex as well as I can do simple.

PEEL the prawns, leaving on the tails.
CUT the salmon into four cubes.
RUB the prawns and salmon with a little sea salt.
CUT the mangetout and mushrooms in half.
DIVIDE the prawns, salmon, mangetout and mushrooms evenly among four 200ml ramekins, Chinese bowls or small mugs.
BEAT the eggs lightly, to avoid froth.
STIR in the dashi, mirin and a pinch of sea salt.
STRAIN through a sieve into the ramekins.
SEAL each one tightly with foil.
STEAM over medium heat for 9 to 10 minutes until smooth, creamy and a little jiggly.
TOP with coriander leaves.
SERVE with spoons.

PRAWN AND SPINACH
dumplings

SERVES 4 / MAKES 16

100g spinach, well washed
400g peeled raw prawns
1 tbsp grated fresh ginger
1 garlic clove, crushed
½ tsp sea salt
1 tsp caster sugar
½ tsp sesame oil
1 tbsp cornflour
1 egg white, well beaten
1 packet square won ton skins

TO SERVE

soy sauce
chilli sauce

It takes years for a dim sum master chef to perfect his exquisite little dumplings. I can't wait that long, so I've come up with a simple version I can make whenever I crave *yum cha*.

TOSS the spinach in a hot dry pan over high heat until just wilted.

COOL, squeeze dry and chop.

WHIZ the prawns in a food processor with the ginger, garlic, sea salt, sugar, sesame oil and cornflour.

ADD the egg white and whiz.

CHILL in the fridge for 1 hour.

SET your steamer going on high.

LINE the rack with baking paper pierced with a skewer.

PLACE 1 heaped tsp filling on each won ton skin.

TOP with 1 tsp spinach.

MOISTEN the edges with a finger dipped in water.

GATHER the edges up over the filling, squeezing gently to form an open dumpling.

STEAM for 8 minutes until firm.

SERVE with soy and chilli sauce for dipping.

SHELLFISH
with rocket pesto

SERVES 4

400g baby new potatoes
(about 12)
600g asparagus, trimmed
1kg fresh shellfish, eg prawns,
langoustines (scampi), crab,
cleaned

ROCKET PESTO:

2 anchovy fillets
50g wild rocket leaves (or wild
garlic shoots in season)
1 hard-boiled egg yolk
1 tbsp freshly grated parmesan
100ml olive oil
2 tsp red wine vinegar

Steaming at its simplest – take fresh shellfish, baby potatoes and asparagus, steam and then serve with a light, rich, creamy pesto.

CHOP the anchovies, rocket and egg yolk for the pesto.
PLACE in a blender with the parmesan, olive oil and red wine vinegar.
WHIZ until you have a mossy green purée.
LIGHTEN with a little water if the pesto is too thick.
REFRIGERATE until needed.
SET a two-level steamer going on high.
STEAM the potatoes for 15 minutes.
ADD the asparagus to the potatoes.
ARRANGE the shellfish in the upper basket.
STEAM both for 4 to 5 minutes, but do not overcook.
SERVE with the rocket pesto for dipping.

CARROT AND CASHEW
nut rice

SERVES 4

1 tbsp vegetable oil

1 small onion, finely diced

1 tsp coriander seeds

1 tsp cumin seeds

1 tbsp mustard seeds

1 tsp ground coriander

1 tsp turmeric

250g freshly grated carrot

250g basmati rice, rinsed

1 tsp sea salt

50g cashew nuts, roasted

fresh flat parsley leaves

1 lemon, quartered

Electric rice-cookers are brilliant, but I still think the best way of cooking rice is simply steaming it in a lidded saucepan – mainly because you can throw in all sorts of things and turn it into a complete meal.

HEAT the oil in a saucepan and cook the onion until soft.

ADD the coriander, cumin and mustard seeds, ground coriander and turmeric and cook for 1 minute.

ADD the grated carrot, stirring well.

TIP in the rice, pour in 500ml water and add the sea salt.

BRING to the boil, stirring.

COVER tightly, trapping a sheet of foil between the pan and lid to seal.

STEAM very gently, undisturbed, for 15 minutes.

LEAVE off the heat, still covered, for 10 minutes.

FLUFF up the rice with two forks.

SCATTER with cashew nuts and parsley leaves.

SERVE with lemon wedges for squeezing.

TEA SPICED
pears

SERVES 4

1 tbsp jasmine tea leaves

150g unrefined brown sugar

4 pears

2 slices fresh ginger

2 cinnamon sticks

2 star anise

1 tbsp goji berries (optional)

Steamed in tea with warming ginger and Asian spices, this is almost like a Chinese *tong sui*, or sweet soup. Unexpected bonus: it makes the kitchen smell divine.

PUT the tea leaves and sugar into a bowl and pour on 1 litre boiling water, stirring.

LEAVE for 10 minutes.

SET your steamer going on high.

PEEL the pears, cut in half and scoop out the cores.

PLACE in a heatproof bowl and strain the tea over them.

ADD the ginger, cinnamon, star anise and goji berries.

STEAM for 20 minutes until the pears are tender.

TRANSFER the pears to serving bowls.

STRAIN the tea into a pan, reserving the spices, and boil until reduced by half.

POUR the tea over the pears and scatter with the reserved spices.

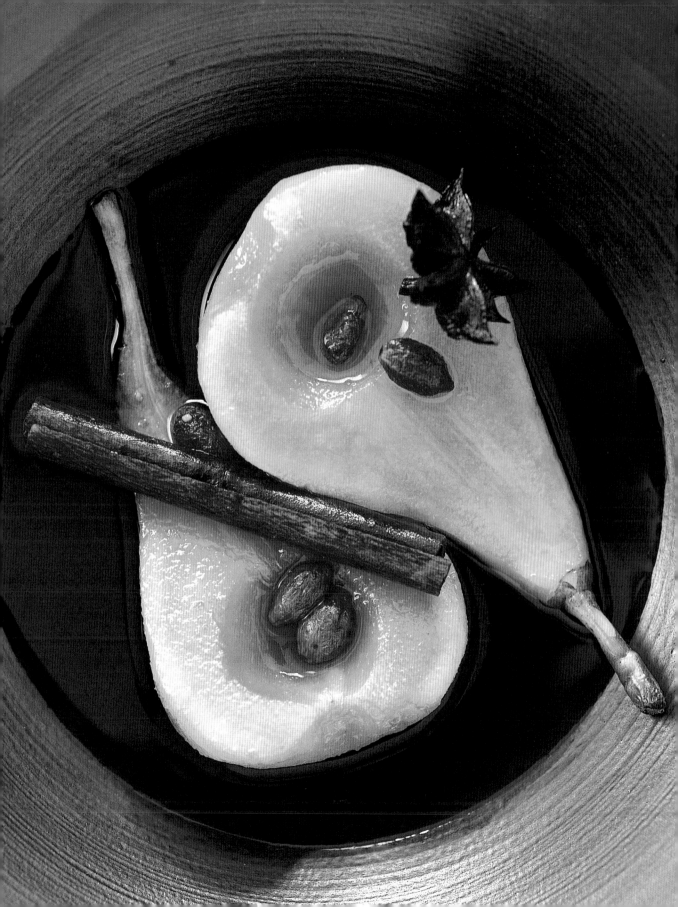

LITTLE FRUITY
puddings

SERVES 6

150g sultanas

150g currants

100ml honey

100g butter, chopped

1 tsp ground mixed spice

1 tsp ground cinnamon

1 tsp ground ginger

200ml strong tea, strained

2 eggs, beaten

200g plain flour

1 tsp baking powder

icing sugar to dust

2 tbsp mostarda di frutta (mustard fruits in syrup) or candied fruits, chopped

Everyone loves a steamed pud and these are small, light and fruity enough to not weigh you down. They also make a light, bright alternative to Christmas pudding.

SET your steamer going on medium.

COMBINE the sultanas, currants, honey, butter, spices and tea in a pan.

BRING to the boil, stirring well, then set aside until cool.

ADD the eggs one at a time, mixing well.

SIFT the flour and baking powder together over the mixture and beat well until evenly combined.

SPOON the mixture into 6 small buttered heatproof pots, to three-quarters fill them.

SEAL tightly with foil and tie with string.

BAKE for 30 minutes or until a thin skewer inserted in the centre comes out clean.

TURN out and dust with icing sugar.

TOP with mustard fruits or candied fruit.

DRIZZLE with the mustard fruit syrup or honey and serve.

Some tools really help you lighten up in the kitchen. Buy a few **plastic squeezy bottles** and decant your every day olive oil into one. Sounds cheffy, but it's all about portion control and precision. Use to oil pans and baking tins, and for that final swirl over grilled fish or soup. From day one, you will use less oil. Use the other bottles for aged balsamic vinegar, honey or this **EASY CARAMEL SAUCE:** place 200ml natural yoghurt and 2 tbsp soft brown sugar in a squeezy bottle and leave for 10 minutes to dissolve the sugar. Shake well and swirl over fruit, cakes and puds.

The old-fashioned **potato ricer** should make a comeback to help us all lighten up. It pushes cooked potatoes, root veg or apples through a mesh of tiny holes, turning them into light, creamy clouds of goodness. Again, it makes a little appear a lot, and gives you incredibly light, fluffy mash without all the butter and milk. For **MUSTARD MASH:** Cook 600g potatoes in boiling salted water until tender. Drain and push through a potato ricer into a bowl. Beat in 1 tbsp grain mustard, sea salt and pepper and spoon back into the ricer. Rice the potatoes directly onto each plate and serve. For 4.

TOOLS X4

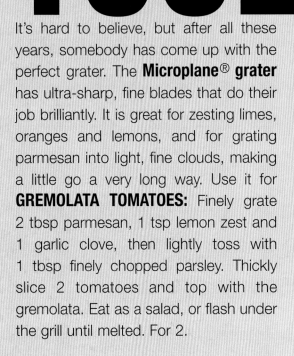

It's hard to believe, but after all these years, somebody has come up with the perfect grater. The **Microplane® grater** has ultra-sharp, fine blades that do their job brilliantly. It is great for zesting limes, oranges and lemons, and for grating parmesan into light, fine clouds, making a little go a very long way. Use it for **GREMOLATA TOMATOES:** Finely grate 2 tbsp parmesan, 1 tsp lemon zest and 1 garlic clove, then lightly toss with 1 tbsp finely chopped parsley. Thickly slice 2 tomatoes and top with the gremolata. Eat as a salad, or flash under the grill until melted. For 2.

Sometimes, it's the little things that make all the difference – even something as simple as a **wooden paddle**, a broad wooden spoon with a square end. It's tailor-made for sauces, stir-fries and the **PERFECT SCRAMBLED EGGS:** Lightly whisk 4 eggs with 60ml skimmed milk, sea salt and pepper. Melt 1 tsp butter in a fry pan over medium heat, add the eggs and leave for 20 seconds. Use the paddle to push the eggs around the pan, leave for 15 seconds, then push again, sweeping the big, soft curds in front without breaking them up. Remove while still soft and scatter with chives. For 2.

SPECIAL
FOOD

I used to worry about inviting people for dinner, until I realised that I was doing it all wrong. I was trying to impress them rather than feed them. Now I just cook what I feel like eating, put the food out and have a good time.

I don't know why we go overboard when we are cooking for friends, as most people love a more relaxed meal of simple food, good wine and lots of talking. It's better to cook something simple and casual for friends once a fortnight, than something complicated and formal, once a year.

Midweek, I find people really appreciate it when I serve something light, like fish and seafood, and put out bowls of vegetables and salad greens. I love serving everything in the middle of the table, and telling everyone to help themselves. That way, people who want huge helpings and those who prefer to pick can do what they like.

It's the same with wine. Rather than dictate the order, vintage and grape variety, I open a red and a white, put them on the table and let everyone sort it out.

Even on the weekend, when there is more time to shop and chop, I'm not comfortable doing anything too formal. It's probably because I am Australian, but I love that mix of being serious about the food and casual about everything else, because it helps people to relax.

We usually start by hanging out in the kitchen, having a glass of bubbly and a nibble instead of sitting down to a first course. I might get someone to toss the salad or set the table. People always prefer to do something, rather than just sit there admiring your furniture while you're in the kitchen pimping their canapés.

To finish, I go for something I can do ahead, like a fabulous chocolate cake, a coffee granita, or a great cheese with juicy, dried fruits and nuts. When I really can't decide what to do, I don't do anything except visit a couple of good shops, and put out a big platter of dark, rich chocolate, wedges of light Italian panettone, crisp little biscotti to soak in a glass of sweet wine, whole clumps of dried muscatels, fat Medjool dates in their little paper cases, and whole nuts for cracking. Everyone lights up as if it's a birthday party, but the interesting thing is that they don't actually overeat, they just have what they want.

There are ideas here for Christmas and birthday dinners, and for whenever you want to make someone feel special, by cooking them a dreamy risotto or a gorgeous soufflé on the spot.

You just have to know what you have time to cook and what you don't have time for. And if anyone asks if there is anything they can do to help, say yes.

CRAB SALAD
with pumpernickel crisps

SERVES 4

1 ripe tomato
2 tbsp extra virgin olive oil
pinch of dried chilli flakes
1 tbsp salted capers, rinsed
2 tsp grated lemon zest
1 tbsp lemon juice, or more
1 tbsp torn basil leaves
sea salt and pepper
300g fresh cooked crabmeat,
  picked over
handful of mâche or rocket
4 slices pumpernickel bread
1 lemon, quartered

It's always hard to come up with something crisp and crunchy that isn't deep-fried, salty or junky. Enter my new favourite nibble with drinks: crisp, toasted, low-GI wholegrain pumpernickel bread.

CUT the tomato in half, squeeze out and discard the seeds and juice, and finely chop the flesh.
PLACE in a bowl and add the olive oil, chilli, capers, lemon zest, lemon juice, basil, sea salt and pepper.
ADD the crabmeat and mâche and lightly toss.
TOAST or grill the pumpernickel bread until crisp.
TOP with the crab salad and serve as an appetiser or first course, with lemon wedges for squeezing.

BALSAMIC PEARS
with prosciutto

SERVES 4

200g sugar

100ml balsamic vinegar, plus
   extra to serve

2 bay leaves

10 black peppercorns

4 tall pears (eg Conference)

4 slices prosciutto

handful of microleaves or
   mustard cress

2 tbsp pine nuts, toasted

1 tbsp extra virgin olive oil

This unusual first course works because a good aged balsamic vinegar is as sweet as it is sour. I stole (or rather borrowed) the idea from talented South Australian chef Genevieve Harris.

PUT the sugar, balsamic vinegar, 500ml water, the bay leaves and peppercorns in a medium pan.

BRING to the boil, stirring to dissolve the sugar.

PEEL the pears and trim the bases, so they sit straight.

SIMMER the pears gently in the syrup for 10 minutes until just tender.

REMOVE from the heat and leave to cool.

HEAT the oven to 180°C/Gas 4.

DRAIN the pears and place on a foil-lined baking tray.

WRAP each one with a furl of prosciutto.

BAKE for 3 to 4 minutes until the prosciutto is crisp.

PLACE the pears on four dinner plates.

SCATTER the leaves and pine nuts around each pear.

DRIZZLE with a little olive oil and balsamic vinegar.

SALMON WITH
rocket and tagliatelle

SERVES 4

400g salmon fillet, skinned

4 vine-ripened tomatoes

300g dried tagliatelle

sea salt and pepper

3 tbsp extra virgin olive oil

1 tbsp grated lemon zest

1 tbsp salted capers, rinsed

1 tbsp lemon juice

2 handfuls of wild rocket leaves

Pasta used to be drowned in creamy sauces in the name of luxury – but the new luxury is to make it chic, glamorous and fresh, without the dairy.

SLICE the salmon into 2cm cubes.

CUT the tomatoes in half, squeeze out the seeds, then cut into small chunks.

COOK the tagliatelle in a large pot of boiling salted water until al dente.

COMBINE the olive oil, salmon, lemon zest, capers, sea salt and pepper in a large fry pan.

COOK gently without 'frying' until the salmon turns pink.

ADD the lemon juice, tomatoes and rocket and toss well.

DRAIN the pasta and gently toss with the salmon.

BUTTERNUT RISOTTO
with goat cheese

SERVES 4

2 butternut squash (unpeeled)

1 tbsp olive oil, plus extra for
  brushing

1 small onion, finely chopped

300g risotto rice

150ml dry white wine

1.5 litres hot vegetable stock,
  heated

sea salt and pepper

freshly grated nutmeg

1 tbsp butter

2 tbsp freshly grated parmesan

150ml goat cheese, sliced

8 small sage leaves

handful of baby salad leaves

Instead of cooking a different meal for the token vegetarian at your table, make a special veggo risotto for everybody. This one is festive enough to serve on Christmas Day.

HEAT the oven to 200°C/Gas 6.

CUT the butternut squash into 3cm thick rounds.

BRUSH with olive oil and bake for 40 minutes.

HEAT the olive oil in a pan and cook the onion until soft.

ADD the unwashed rice, stirring well.

POUR in the wine and let it bubble away as you stir.

ADD the hot stock gradually, a ladleful at a time, stirring, until the rice is tender and creamy but not soft, about 30 minutes.

SET aside four pumpkin rounds for serving.

SKIN the rest and roughly chop, discarding the seeds.

ADD to the risotto with sea salt, pepper, nutmeg, butter and parmesan, and heat through.

SPOON the risotto on top of the roast pumpkin rounds.

TOP with goat cheese and freshly ground pepper.

SCATTER with sage and salad leaves, then serve.

SPICE-CRUSTED VENISON
with beetroot

SERVES 4

1 tsp black peppercorns

1 tsp juniper berries

1 tsp caraway seeds

sea salt and pepper

4 thin venison steaks,
  180g each

1 tbsp olive oil for brushing

400g cooked beetroot, peeled

150ml red wine

2 tbsp cranberry or redcurrant
  jelly

200g watercress, washed

Young, lean, clean-flavoured venison is cooked fast until crusty on the outside and tender inside. The new three-minute steak, it's the red meat of the future.

CRUSH the peppercorns, juniper berries, caraway seeds and 1 tsp sea salt and scatter on a plate.

BRUSH the venison steaks with olive oil.

PRESS one side of each steak into the spices.

HEAT a non-stick fry pan.

PLACE the steaks, spiced-side down, in the pan.

COOK over a high heat for 2 minutes.

TURN and cook the other side for 1 minute, depending on thickness, leaving the inside pink.

TRANSFER to a warm plate to rest.

CUT the beetroot into small dice and add to the pan.

POUR in the wine and boil for 30 seconds, stirring well.

ADD the jelly, sea salt and pepper and stir until syrupy.

SLICE the venison and arrange on a platter with the glazed beetroot.

SCATTER with watercress and serve.

PINEAPPLE
and coconut soufflé

SERVES 4

3 tbsp desiccated coconut

1 tbsp butter

3 large eggs (65 to 70g),
separated

100g caster sugar

200g canned crushed pineapple,
drained, or puréed fresh
pineapple

1 tbsp icing sugar

This is a very elegant and non-scary sort of soufflé, made only with crushed pineapple, eggs, sugar and nutty toasted coconut.

HEAT the oven to 190°C/Gas 5.

SCATTER the coconut on a baking tray and toast in the oven for 1 minute until golden.

BUTTER four 250ml soufflé dishes.

BEAT the egg yolks and half the sugar together in a bowl until pale.

STIR in the pineapple, then 2 tbsp of the coconut.

BEAT the egg whites in a clean bowl to firm peaks.

ADD the remaining sugar to the egg whites and beat well until thick and glossy.

FOLD into the pineapple mixture with a light hand.

FILL the soufflé dishes to the brim and smooth the tops.

BAKE for 10 minutes until risen and lightly golden.

DUST with icing sugar, scatter with the remaining toasted coconut and serve immediately.

COFFEE
granita

SERVES 4

40g ground espresso coffee
100g sugar
½ tsp vanilla extract
100g thick Greek yoghurt to
  serve (optional)
1 tsp instant coffee (optional)

I became addicted to this one very hot summer in Rome, when coffee was too hot and gelati was too rich. Pass a chilled bottle of your favourite Italian liqueur around the table to drizzle over the top.

MAKE your espresso coffee, using 400ml boiling water.
ADD the sugar and vanilla while the espresso is hot, stirring until dissolved.
LEAVE to cool.
POUR into a freezerproof metal container.
FREEZE for 2 hours or until partly frozen.
SCRAPE with a fork to break up the crystals and refreeze.
BREAK up the crystals every hour for 3 hours.
SPOON the granita into four chilled small glasses.
TOP with a plop of yoghurt, sprinkle with instant coffee if you like, and serve immediately.

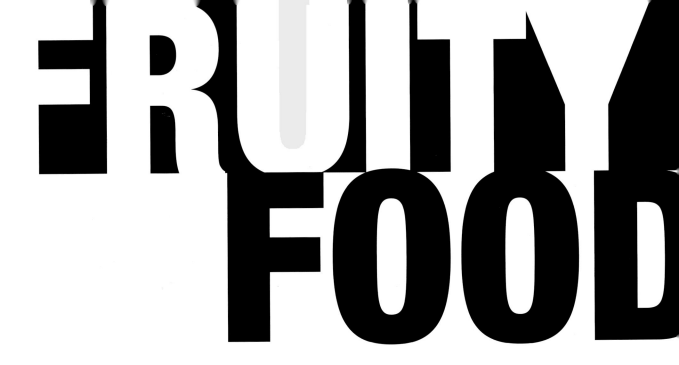

We all love desserts, and we don't eat enough fruit, so it makes sense to combine the two. Fruit is the lightest, brightest way to end a meal, either in its own right, or as a way of freshening up something sweet or cakey.

Fruit is also nice and quick, which is handy for those times you didn't think you were going to have a pud, but changed your mind at the last minute. And it is *so* good for you. Berries and pomegranates, in particular, are loaded with the antioxidants we need for healthy skin (and a healthy body, but that's by the by) so we should eat them out of mere vanity and not just greed.

When I eat out, I can't believe how many dessert menus completely overlook fruit. At home, my kitchen is full of either ripening pears or perfect peaches queuing up for me to eat, and all I get when I go out is a crème caramel or a crème brûlée. As my favourite restaurant critic Terry Durack says, "the first 500 crème brulées are wonderful. The next 500 get a little boring." But fresh fruit changes all year round and can't possibly be monotonous.

I almost weep at the end of summer when I have to say goodbye to all my cherries, raspberries and melons. But then I get so used to my crisp mid-afternoon apple, refreshing mandarin juice cocktails and after-dinner treats of a juicy pear and a wedge of Parmigiano Reggiano, that I feel like crying at the end of winter, too.

Puds are all about our childhood, and feeling warm and loved. Adults turn into big kids at the sight of a great dessert, and I love coming up with different ways of turning fruit into something special – like whizzing frozen bananas into rich, creamy, ice-creams, or transforming berries into sparkling chilled soups with red wine.

They are treats, and treats have a role in a balanced diet – otherwise it wouldn't be balanced. Even creamy desserts and steamy puddings should be revelled in, without a large helping of guilt on the side. Just turn them into small pleasures (like the cupcake, portion control at its cutest) and enjoy a pudding when you really feel like one, not as a daily habit. That's what 'moderation' is all about.

And if you love cream, feel free to add a spoonful. I don't because I don't particularly like cream, or perhaps I just lost the taste for it when I discovered tangy, low-fat yoghurt, rich in live, active cultures. (Natural is best, as the fruit versions contain either sugar or artificial sweeteners – you can always add a touch of honey or maple syrup if you find it is too sharp.) For me, yoghurt is just as rich and creamy, but it feels lighter and silkier. And surely that means I can have more pud.

RASPBERRY
éclairs

SERVES 4

6 firm ripe bananas

150g raspberries or strawberries

8 sponge finger (savoiardi)
biscuits

100g raspberries to serve

This creamy berry ice-cream is made without eggs, sugar or cream – just fruit. Sandwich between sponge fingers, wafers or those cute little sesame snap wafers.

PEEL the bananas and roughly chop.

WASH the berries; hull the strawberries and cut in half if large.

PLACE the bananas and berries in a freezer bag.

FREEZE overnight until solid.

SOFTEN at room temperature for 15 to 20 minutes.

WHIZ in a food processor until smooth and creamy.

SERVE now as a soft-serve ice-cream, or freeze in a plastic container for 3 hours until firm.

SOFTEN for 10 minutes out of the freezer.

SCOOP onto four sponge fingers and sandwich with the remaining fingers.

SCATTER with berries and serve.

MOCK CHOC
ice-cream

SERVES 4

8 firm ripe bananas

2 tbsp cocoa powder, sifted

50g dark bitter chocolate
  (70% cocoa solids)

100g cherries to serve

The berry ice-cream on the previous page is so good, I've included a chocky version as well. Pile it into glasses and drizzle with chocolate, or freeze overnight for an ice-cream you can scoop or slice.

PEEL the bananas and roughly chop.

SEAL in a plastic bag and freeze overnight.

SOFTEN for 15 to 20 minutes out of the freezer.

WHIZ in a food processor until thick, smooth and creamy.

ADD the cocoa powder and whiz again until smooth.

PILE into four chilled glasses.

CHOP the chocolate into shards.

SCATTER the ice-cream with chocolate and cherries and serve immediately.

HOT ROAST
fruit salad

SERVES 4

4 small red apples
2 pears
½ lemon
butter to grease
250ml white wine or water
2 cinnamon sticks
2 tbsp soft brown sugar
2 firm figs
2 clementines or mandarins
100g blueberries

Roasting intensifies all the mellow flavours of autumn and winter fruits. Serve with butterscotch yoghurt cream (page 215) for an extra treat.

HEAT the oven to 180°C/Gas 4.

SLIT the skin of each apple from top to bottom.

HALVE the pears lengthways, remove the core with a melon baller and drizzle with lemon juice.

ARRANGE the apples and pears in a baking tray lined with buttered baking paper.

POUR in the wine and add the cinnamon sticks.

SCATTER the sugar over the fruit.

BAKE for 30 minutes.

CUT the figs and clementines in half.

ADD to the baking tray and bake for 10 minutes.

ADD the blueberries and toss to coat them in the warm pan juices.

SERVE warm, drizzled with the sweet, fruity pan juices.

PERSIAN
rice pud

SERVES 4

butter for pots
180g arborio (risotto) rice
1 litre milk
1 cinnamon stick
100g caster sugar
2 egg yolks, beaten
1 tbsp rose water
1 pomegranate, seeds extracted
silver dragees to serve (optional)

Exotic, scarlet-skinned pomegranates – one of nature's superfoods – hide hundreds of juicy, jewel-like seeds. Cut into quarters and push out the seeds with your fingers, or top the puds with berries or dried fruits.

BUTTER four small pudding bowls or moulds lightly.
HEAT the rice, milk and cinnamon stick in a pan.
BRING to the boil, stirring, then lower the heat.
SIMMER gently, stirring occasionally, for 20 minutes or until the rice is tender and has absorbed the milk.
REMOVE from the heat and stir in the sugar.
BEAT in the egg yolks and rose water, mixing thoroughly.
SPOON into the bowls or moulds and allow to cool.
CHILL in the fridge overnight.
UNMOULD onto serving plates.
SCATTER with pomegranate seeds and silver dragees.

RED WINE
and berry soup

SERVES 4

RED WINE SLUSH:

500g strawberries, hulled
100ml Pinot Noir or light red wine
150g sugar

BERRY SOUP:

200g raspberries
100g blackberries
100g blueberries
200ml Pinot Noir or light red wine
50g caster sugar
2 tbsp orange juice
a few basil and mint leaves
zest of 1 orange

We all have to make hay while the sun shines. I take that to mean eating a lot of fresh, juicy berries in an icy slush of red wine on the hottest days of summer.

TOSS the strawberries with the red wine and sugar.

LEAVE to macerate for 1 hour.

WHIZ to a purée and pour into a freezerproof container.

FREEZE for 2 hours until firm.

CRUSH half of the raspberries and blackberries for the berry soup.

ADD the whole berries, red wine, sugar and orange juice.

LEAVE to macerate for 2 hours.

SPOON the berry soup into pretty glass bowls.

BEAT the red wine slush to break up the ice crystals.

STIR the slush into the soup to thicken and chill it.

SCATTER with basil, mint and orange zest.

VERY BERRY
puds

SERVES 4 TO 6

125g butter, softened, plus
  extra for pots
125g caster sugar
2 eggs, at room temperature
125g plain flour
1 tsp baking powder
80ml milk
300g mixed berries (eg
  blackberries and raspberries)
150ml port
50g sugar

Life would be miserable without an occasional little steamed pudding to make you feel good – especially one bursting with berries in a boozy sauce.

HEAT the oven to 180°C/Gas 4.
BUTTER four individual heatproof pudding bowls or pots.
BEAT the butter and caster sugar together in a bowl until light and fluffy.
BEAT in the eggs, one at a time.
SIFT the flour and baking powder together.
FOLD into the mix, alternately with the milk, until smooth.
PUT a layer of berries in the base of each mould.
TOP with the mixture to three-quarters fill the moulds.
SEAL tightly with foil and tie with string.
STAND in a baking tray and surround with boiling water to come halfway up the sides.
BAKE for 35 to 40 minutes until springy to the touch.
HEAT remaining berries with port and sugar until soft.
TURN out the puddings onto rimmed plates.
SPOON the berry sauce over the top and serve.

PLUM SALAD
with cranberry jelly

SERVES 4

4 gelatine leaves
500ml cranberry juice
100g caster sugar
4 fresh ripe plums
150g blueberries

A ripe and juicy plum, peach or nectarine is a divine summer treat on its own – and it's even more divine with a juicy little jelly scattered on top.

SOAK the gelatine leaves in cold water for 5 minutes.

HEAT the cranberry juice and sugar in a pan, stirring.

TAKE off the heat.

SQUEEZE out excess water from the gelatine, then whisk into the hot liquid until melted.

POUR into a shallow baking tin, cover and chill overnight.

CUT the plums into 1cm slices, removing the stones.

ARRANGE on four plates.

TURN out the jelly and chop into small dice.

SCATTER the cranberry jelly and blueberries over the plums and serve.

SAGO PUD
with mango

SERVES 4

150g pearl sago (small seed)
80g soft brown unrefined sugar
  or palm sugar
100ml thick coconut milk
pinch of salt
1 ripe mango

Pearl sago has a slippery-slide quality you either love or hate. But even people who hate it might like it with fresh mango, brown sugar syrup and coconut cream.

BRING a pan of water to the boil.
ADD the sago slowly, stirring as you go.
COOK, stirring occasionally, for 15 minutes until soft.
HEAT the sugar and 100ml water in a pan, stirring to dissolve.
SIMMER for 5 minutes to reduce to a syrup.
DRAIN the sago, rinse under cold water and drain well.
TIP into a bowl and add half the sugar syrup, half the coconut milk and the salt.
MIX well and pour into four individual pots or ramekins.
COVER and chill for a few hours.
CUT 2 cheeks from the mango, slice the flesh lengthways and peel.
TURN out the puddings onto individual plates.
DRIZZLE with the remaining syrup and coconut milk.
ARRANGE the mango slices alongside and serve.

LEMON YOGHURT
cupcakes

MAKES 10

125g butter, softened
125g caster sugar
3 eggs, separated
1 tbsp finely grated lemon zest
2 tbsp lemon juice
180g plain flour
1 tsp baking powder
200ml natural yoghurt
4 tbsp icing sugar
dash of lemon juice
100g mixed berries
1 tbsp lemon zest

When you really feel like cake, these cute, little, not-too-sweet cupcakes will do the trick. Top with a smudge of lemon icing and fresh fruits.

HEAT the oven to 180°C/Gas 4.

SET 10 paper muffin cases in a large muffin tray.

BEAT the butter and sugar together until pale and fluffy.

ADD the egg yolks one at a time, beating well.

BEAT in the lemon zest and juice.

SIFT the flour and baking powder together.

FOLD into the cake mixture, alternating with the yoghurt.

WHISK the egg whites in a clean bowl to firm peaks.

FOLD into the mixture.

FILL the paper cases.

BAKE for 30 minutes or until a skewer inserted into the centre of a muffin comes out clean.

COOL on a wire rack.

MIX the icing sugar with a little lemon juice to make a thick icing.

SPREAD on top of the cakes, add a berry or two or some lemon zest, and leave to set.

EXTRAS

But wait, there's more...here are a few back-to-basics extras to help you lighten up your cooking, from the stock at the very foundation, to the dressing on top. All recipes serve 4 unless I say otherwise.

The best way to add flavour to your cooking is with a home-made broth, or stock. It gives you a huge head start over cooking in boring old water, and when it is reduced (by long simmering), it makes a great, fat-free sauce for meats and fish. To make a **SIMPLE VEGETABLE STOCK:** roughly chop 3 onions, 3 carrots and 3 celery stalks and toss into a large stock pot with 3 parsley stems (not leaves). Cover with 2 litres cold water, bring to the boil and simmer, uncovered, for 1 hour. Strain and use for soups, risotto and sauces. If you are short on time, I recommend using Marigold Organic Swiss Vegetable Bouillon Powder, which tastes fresh and carroty.

Make your own light, subtle, fragrant **JAPANESE DASHI BROTH** by simmering konbu (giant kelp) and dried bonito fish. Slowly bring 30g konbu and 1 litre cold water to a simmer in a pan and simmer for 10 minutes without boiling. Add 30g dried bonito flakes, simmer for 5 minutes and strain through muslin or a fine sieve.

INSTANT DASHI is even easier. Bring 1 litre water to the boil. Add 10g sachet of dashi powder (from Japanese food stores and health food stores), simmer for 2 minutes and use.

To turn dashi broth into a rich, savoury **MISO BROTH:** add 1 tbsp mirin and 1 tbsp soy sauce. Whisk 1 generous tbsp miso paste into 2 tbsp of the broth, then pour back into the soup, whisking.

To make your own **CHICKEN STOCK:** rinse 2kg chicken bones, put into a large pot and cover with 4 litres cold water. Bring to the boil then simmer for 10 minutes, skimming off any froth. Add 2 halved and finely sliced onions, 2 roughly chopped carrots, 2 roughly chopped celery stalks and 2 finely chopped leeks. Simmer for 2 hours, skimming occasionally. Strain, discarding the vegetables and bones, and leave to cool. Refrigerate overnight, then remove any fat that has risen to the surface. Keep the stock in the fridge if using within a day or two, otherwise freeze until needed.

To make a fast **TOMATO SUGO** for those times you desperately need spaghetti al pomodoro: in a pan, combine 400g canned chopped tomatoes with 1 tbsp olive oil, 2 crushed garlic cloves, sea salt, a pinch of sugar, 1/2 tsp dried oregano, 1 tbsp salted capers (rinsed), and some basil leaves if there are any around. Simmer for 20 minutes until thick.

Make your own vivid green **PESTO** to add to soups, vegetables, breads and pasta: whiz 2 cups (60g) fresh basil leaves with 2 crushed garlic cloves, a good pinch of sea salt, 2 tbsp toasted pine nuts, and 2 tbsp freshly grated parmesan in a blender. Gradually add 200ml olive oil, whizzing. Store in an airtight jar in the fridge, and top up with olive oil as you use the pesto, to seal it.

Come up with your own **HOUSE DRESSING:** an all-purpose vinaigrette for salads and vegetables. Here's mine: in a large bowl, whisk together 1 tbsp red wine vinegar, 1 tsp Dijon mustard, 2 tbsp extra virgin olive oil, sea salt and freshly ground black pepper to taste. The mustard will thicken the dressing naturally, so I then lighten it by whisking in one of the following: 1 tbsp mirin (sweet Japanese rice wine), whatever white wine is in the fridge door, thin yoghurt, apple juice, water, or the squishy juices of a fresh, ripe tomato.

For a brilliant **TAHINI DRESSING**: beat or whiz 2 tbsp tahini (sesame seed paste), with 1 crushed garlic clove, ½ tsp sea salt, ½ tsp ground cumin, 2 tbsp lemon juice and 4 tbsp water, until smooth. Add a little extra water or yoghurt until the sauce is thick but runny, and drizzle over grills, roasts, salads and almost anything involving aubergine.

I don't eat a lot of mayonnaise but when I do I want it to be garlicky, golden, home-made aïoli. To make 300ml **AIOLI**: whiz 2 whole egg yolks, 1 crushed garlic clove, 1 tsp Dijon mustard, ½ tsp salt and 2 tbsp lemon juice in a blender or processor. Very slowly, at a bare trickle, add 100ml grapeseed oil, then 100ml olive oil (or 200ml good light olive oil) whizzing until the aïoli is thick, smooth and silky. Beat in 1 tbsp boiling water and refrigerate. Serve with le grand aïoli (page 162), and with garlicky prawns, grilled fish, asparagus, seafood soups, hard-boiled eggs, roast pork, tomato salads and veggie stews.

For a crunchy **MEXICAN SALSA CRUDA** to lighten up eggs, grills, beans and tacos: finely dice 2 ripe tomatoes and ½ red onion. Mix with 1 finely chopped red chilli, 2 tbsp chopped coriander, sea salt and a squeeze of lime or orange juice. Serve now or keep on going, adding some finely chopped red or green pepper, avocado or pickled jalapeño chillies if you so desire.

For a devilishly spicy **AJVAR RELISH** of smoky aubergine and red pepper from Eastern Europe: toss 2 aubergines and 2 sweet red peppers with 1 tbsp olive oil in a roasting pan and bake at 200°C/Gas 6 for 30 minutes. Cool slightly, then roughly chop into chunks, discarding the seeds and cores from the peppers. Mix the chopped vegetables with 2 tbsp olive oil, 1 tbsp lemon juice, sea salt, pepper and a pinch of cayenne. Serve as it is, or whiz to a coarse purée. Brilliant for barbecues or with anything grilled, like cevapcici sausages (page 75).

PERFECT STEAMED RICE is beautifully simple if you use the rule-of-thumb method, or specifically, forefinger: rinse 300g basmati or fragrant jasmine rice well under cold running water, drain, and toss it into a heavy-based pot. Rest your forefinger on the surface of the rice, and add cold water until it reaches to the first knuckle (around 2cm). Bring to the boil, cover tightly, and simmer on the lowest possible heat for 18 minutes. Leave, covered, off the heat for 5 minutes, then fluff up the rice with a fork before serving. (If you are worried about your finger being too long or too short, then add 550ml water instead).

To make **YOGHURT ICE-CREAM** whisk 500g thick, Greek-style yoghurt with 50g icing sugar, then churn in an ice-cream machine according to the manufacturer's instructions. Otherwise, freeze the yoghurt mixture for 1 hour, beating three times at 30 minute intervals to break up the ice crystals, then freeze until firm. Soften for 20 minutes and serve with toasted walnuts and honey.

For a **BUTTERSCOTCH YOGHURT CREAM** to dollop over fresh fruits, cakes and puddings: place 300g natural yoghurt in a shallow bowl and scatter with 2 tbsp soft brown unrefined sugar. Leave for about 15 minutes to dissolve, then swirl the melted sugar through the yoghurt. Who needs cream?

Make a refreshing **HOME-MADE LEMONADE** for summer picnics and mid-afternoon pick-me-ups: Combine 100g caster sugar, 150ml water and the grated zest of 1 unwaxed lemon in a saucepan. Bring to the boil, stirring until the sugar is dissolved. Squeeze 2 lemons until you have 100ml juice. Add to the pan and leave to cool. Strain through a coarse strainer and store in a screw-topped or corkable bottle in the fridge until needed. To serve, mix one part lemon syrup to two parts mineral water.

One of the nicest ways to start or finish a meal is with **A FRESH, LIGHT CHEESE**: To make your own, whiz 250g fresh ricotta and 250g whole-milk natural yoghurt in a food processor to a smooth, white purée. Tip into a dampened muslin-lined sieve set over a bowl, then cover and leave in a cool place to drain for 12 hours. Serve with crispbread and olives; or drizzle with lavender or orange flower honey, strew with roasted almonds and serve with ripe melon, a crisp pear or some cherries.

GLOSSARY

ARBORIO RICE: A plump superfino rice grown in Northern Italy. Use for risotto and rice puddings.

ASIAN MUSHROOMS: Shimeji grow in clusters of pale, elegant stalks; erynji (king oyster) have long tuber-shaped stems with oyster-shaped caps and a subtle, creamy flavour; nameko is an autumn mushroom, small-capped and slender-stemmed; oyster mushrooms are pale and creamy, shiitake mushrooms are honey brown; and enoki are tiny, white cotton-bud shapes. Available from specialist supermarkets and Japanese food stores.

BONITO FLAKES: Very fine shavings from a bonito, a fish of the mackerel family, which has been smoked, dried and fermented. Used in making dashi stock, and for flavouring Japanese soups. Available from Japanese food stores.

CHILLI BEAN SAUCE: A fiery Sichuan chilli bean paste (*toban djan*) available in jars from Asian food stores.

CHINESE RICE WINE: A yellow rice wine (*shao hsing*) made from glutinous rice, used in marinades, stir-fries and braised dishes. Dry sherry can be substituted.

DAIKON: A large, long white radish, often called mooli in UK. It has a refreshing bite when freshly grated, and a gentle flavour when simmered in soups and stews.

DRIED PORCINI, OR CEPS: Dried Italian or French mushrooms (*boletus edulis*) with a rich, earthy flavour and intense aroma. Great for vegetable stock bases.

EDAMAME: Young soybeans, available par-boiled and snap-frozen. Lightly boil for 5 minutes, and eat straight from the pod. Increasingly available. Small broad beans (fava) can be substituted.

GLASS NOODLES: Also known as cellophane noodles, these are thin, white, dried vermicelli made from mung beans. Soak for 5 minutes before cooking, and snip with scissors into manageable lengths.

GOCHUJANG: A spicy Korean sauce of fermented soybeans, glutinous rice powder and chilli, sold in jars. Can be refrigerated for several months.

GOJI BERRIES: Also known as wolfberries, these are dried red berries – rich in nutrients and antioxidants, with a slightly tart sweet taste. Eat as they are, add to yoghurts and fruits, or simmer to make goji tea.

GREEN TEA: Japanese green tea, like sencha, has six times the antioxidant levels of black tea.

HARISSA: A spicy paste of dried red chillies and garlic. The best is available in jars from speciality food stores. If buying in tubes, dilute with olive oil and taste for strength and coarseness.

HEMP SEEDS (NUTS): The 'sexy' seed is full of essential fatty acids, minerals and proteins, and tastes sweetly nutty, as does hemp seed oil. Buy raw and shelled, and add to salads, cereals, fruit and avocado dishes.

MICROLEAVES: Intensely flavoured baby salad leaves with higher concentrations of phyto-chemicals than in their adult form; eg mizuna, red chard, cress, red perilla, shiso.

MISO: Fermented soybean paste with a rich savoury taste used in Japanese cooking. Add to soups, stews and marinades.

MIRIN: A light, sweet Japanese rice wine with low alcohol content, used for sauces, dressings and marinades.

MOSTARDA DI FRUTTA: Italian mustard fruits, preserved in syrup. Very beautiful, with a slow, stealthy warmth.

NIGELLA SEEDS: Known in India as *kalonji*, these look like black sesame seeds and have a lightly peppery, nutty taste.

NORI: Thin sheets of seaweed with a high protein content. Store in an airtight container or they will go stale. Lightly toast over a flame before using.

PALM SUGAR: A natural sugar formed from the sap of a palm flower.

PAPRIKA: Spanish smoked paprika, which has a rich smoky flavour and good heat levels, is my favourite.

PASSATA: Smooth, thick sieved Italian tomatoes widely used as a sauce base, also known as *sugo di pomodoro*. Available from supermarkets.

PINOT NOIR: Red wine grapes with especially high levels of antioxidants.

PRESERVED LEMONS: Small whole lemons preserved in a salty brine, available from Middle Eastern specialists and major supermarkets. Rinse well, and use only the rind.

QUINOA: A nutritious, gluten-free grain from the Andes that is considered a complete protein. Use as you would cracked (bulghur) wheat.

RICE VINEGAR: A clear, mild vinegar made from fermented rice, from Asian food stores.

ROSE WATER: A clear, light distillation of rose petals. From Middle Eastern stores and major supermarkets.

SAUERKRAUT (CHOUCROUTE): Finely shredded, salted, fermented white cabbage that is high in flavour and vitamins, low on kilojoules.

SEA SALT: Unrefined sea salt is much higher in vital essential minerals than processed salt. Upgrade to Maldon (UK), Fleur de Sel (France) or Murray River (Australia), and use sparingly.

SEAWEED (SEA VEGETABLES): High in calcium, iron and iodine, these are the most nutrient-packed food we have. Buy individual seaweeds (arame, wakame, etc) or mixed packs. Soak in water for 15 minutes and add to soups and salads.

SPROUTS: Highly nutritious baby living plants you can grow at home – from lentils, mung beans, sunflower seeds, chick peas, etc.

SUGAR: Choose natural unrefined sugars, for more flavour and health benefits, or substitute with raw honey or genuine maple syrup.

TAHINI: A thick, creamy, nutty paste with a high calcium content, made from husked and ground sesame seeds. Available in jars from Middle Eastern specialists and health food stores.

TAMARI: A thick soy sauce made without wheat.

TAMARIND: A sour-tasting fruit sold as a pulp or, more conveniently, as a refined concentrate in small jars. Available from Asian food stores and some supermarkets.

TOBIKO: A very fine, crunchy Japanese fish roe, often coloured red, salmon orange or wasabi green. Available frozen from Japanese speciality stores and fishmongers.

TOGARASHI: Popular Japanese seasoning made of dried chilli, sansho pepper, sesame seeds and seaweed. Available from Japanese food stores.

UDON NOODLES: Fat white Japanese noodles made from wheat flour; ideal for soups and casseroles. If they are dried, cook for 8 minutes in simmering water. If vac-packed and ready to eat, rinse in boiling water.

WASABI: A pungent green paste to accompany sushi and sashimi, often called Japanese horseradish. Available as a green powder, a paste in a tube, or fresh.

INDEX

CONVERSIONS

WEIGHT

15g	$^1/_2$oz
20g	$^3/_4$oz
25g	1oz
40g	1$^1/_2$oz
50g	2oz
75g	3oz
100g	3$^1/_2$oz
110g	4oz
125g	4$^1/_2$oz
150g	5oz
175g	6oz
200g	7oz
225g	8oz
250g	9oz
275g	10oz
300g	10$^1/_2$oz
350g	12oz
400g	14oz
425g	15oz
450g	1lb
500g	1lb 2oz
600g	1$^1/_4$lb
700g	1$^1/_2$lb
750g	1lb 10oz
900g	2lb
1kg	2$^1/_4$lb
1.5kg	3$^1/_4$lb
2kg	4$^1/_2$lb

VOLUME

5ml	1 teaspoon (tsp)
10ml	1 dessertspoon (dsp)
15ml	1 tablespoon (tbsp)
20ml	1 Australian tablespoon
30ml	1fl oz
40ml	1$^1/_2$fl oz
60ml	2fl oz
85ml	3fl oz
100ml	3$^1/_2$fl oz
125ml	4fl oz
150ml	5fl oz
175ml	6fl oz
200ml	7fl oz
250ml	8fl oz
300ml	10fl oz ($^1/_2$ pint)
350ml	12fl oz
375ml	13fl oz
400ml	14fl oz
425ml	15fl oz ($^3/_4$ pint)
450ml	16fl oz
500ml	18fl oz
600ml	20fl oz (1 pint)
750ml	1$^1/_4$ pints
800ml	1$^1/_3$ pints
1 litre	1$^3/_4$ pints
1.2 litres	2 pints
1.5 litres	2$^1/_2$ pints
2 litres	3$^1/_2$ pints

LENGTH

5mm	$^1/_4$ inch
1cm	$^1/_2$ inch
2.5cm	1 inch
5cm	2 inch
7.5cm	3 inch
10cm	4 inch
12cm	5 inch
15cm	6 inch
18cm	7 inch
20cm	8 inch
23cm	9 inch
25cm	10 inch
28cm	11 inch
30cm	12 inch

OVEN TEMPERATURES

Cooking times used are based on a conventional oven. If you are using a fan-assisted oven, set the temperature to 10° to 15°C lower than called for in the recipe.

140°C	275°F	Gas 1	Cool
150°C	300°F	Gas 2	Low
160°C	325°F	Gas 3	Moderately low
180°C	350°F	Gas 4	Moderate
190°C	375°F	Gas 5	Moderately hot
200°C	400°F	Gas 6	Hot
220°C	425°F	Gas 7	Hot
230°C	450°F	Gas 8	Very hot

NOTES

Conversions are approximate, either rounded up or down for convenience. Eggs are free-range and medium unless otherwise stated, ie 60g (2oz); herbs are fresh; salt is sea salt, and pepper is freshly ground black pepper unless otherwise suggested. Spoon measures are level: 1 tsp = 5ml spoon; 1 tbsp = 15ml spoon.

THANK YOU

This book was a delight to work on from start to finish, from writing and testing recipes in chilly London to shooting it in sunny Sydney. A big thank you to Alison Cathie and the sales team at Quadrille for their vision; Jane O'Shea and Helen Lewis for master-minding; Katherine Case for her clarity of design; and editor Janet Illsley for her wisdom and patience.

I was very lucky to work with photographer Petrina Tinslay, who brings freshness and light to every page. Thank you, Petrina, from the bottom of my heart. Thanks to both Heidi Flett and Sophie Fitzgerald, for doing what needed to be done before we knew we needed it.

And thank you, super stylist Lynsey Freers for gathering such delicious props from the brilliant designers, cookware, homewares and furniture stores of Sydney and Melbourne. My thanks to you all for allowing me to use your beautiful things: Academy Tiles, Accoutrement Cooking School, All Hand Made Gallery, Anibou, Bison, Bunnings, Country Trader, Crowley and Grouch, De De Ce, Dinosaur Designs, Empire Vintage, Essential Ingredient, Form and Design, Honeybee, Hub, Interstudio, Michael Greene Antiques, Miljo, Mud Australia, No Chintz, Ondene, Orson and Blake (Surry Hills), PAD, Pigott's Store, Porters Paints, Space, Spence and Lyda, Sunbeam, The Art of Food and Wine, The Bay Tree, Thonet, Top 3 by Design, Vicino, Waterford and Wedgwood. I hope I did them all justice.

As for Terry, this book is as much yours as mine. Thank you for all your hard work, your generosity, your Campari and sodas, and your love. You make everything a joy.

PUBLISHING DIRECTOR Jane O'Shea
CREATIVE DIRECTOR Helen Lewis
PROJECT EDITOR Janet Illsley
DESIGNER Katherine Case
PHOTOGRAPHER Petrina Tinslay
FOOD STYLIST Jill Dupleix
PRODUCTION Ruth Deary

This edition first published in 2009 by Quadrille Publishing Limited
Alhambra House
27–31 Charing Cross Road
London WC2H 0LS
www.quadrille.co.uk

Text © 2007 Jill Dupleix
Photography © 2007 Petrina Tinslay
Design and layout © 2007 Quadrille Publishing Limited

The rights of the author have been asserted.
Cataloguing in Publication Data: a catalogue record for this book is available from the British Library.

ISBN: 978 184400 7011

Printed in China